CHAPTER 1:
THE POWER OF COMMUNICATION: MASTERING THE ART OF LONG DISTANCE CONVERSATIONS

Understanding the importance of effective communication in a long distance relationship

Being in a long distance relationship can be challenging, especially when it comes to maintaining a strong connection and intimacy with your partner. The physical distance between you can create barriers that hinder communication and make it difficult to stay connected on an emotional level. However, effective communication is the key to overcoming these challenges and nurturing a healthy and thriving long distance relationship.

In *The Long Distance Relationships Guidebook* we recognize the significance of communication in long distance love and highlights its crucial role in building trust, understanding, and emotional connection. This chapter will explore the importance of effective communication, as well as provide practical tips and strategies to help you master the art of long distance conversations.

The challenges posed by distance on communication in a relationship are numerous and varied. Time zone differences, cultural disparities, and language barriers can all make communication more complex and challenging. However, rather than letting these obstacles discourage you, it is essential to approach them as opportunities for growth and connection.

Clear and consistent communication is the foundation of a successful long distance relationship. By actively engaging in open and honest conversations, you can bridge the gap created by distance and ensure that your partner feels heard, understood, and valued. Good communication not only helps maintain a sense of closeness but also strengthens the trust and understanding between you and your partner.

Throughout this chapter, we emphasize the importance of effective communication techniques to overcome the limitations imposed by distance. Strategies such as scheduling regular check-ins, using technology to bridge the gap, and learning about your partner's culture and language can help break down communication barriers and foster a deeper level of connection.

Active listening skills play a crucial role in ensuring understanding and emotional connection during conversations. By actively listening to your partner's thoughts, feelings, and concerns, you demonstrate empathy and create a safe space for open communication.

Different forms of communication, including phone calls, video chats, and text messaging, offer unique advantages and drawbacks in a long distance relationship. We compare and contrast these forms, helping you identify which ones work best for your particular situation and preferences. Additionally, we provide recommendations for utilizing different forms of communication based on specific circumstances.

Consistency and regularity are essential in maintaining a strong connection with your partner. Setting communication routines and expectations, scheduling regular check-ins, and utilizing shared calendars or online tools can help you maintain consistent and meaningful communication despite time zone differences or busy schedules. We also offer creative suggestions for spicing up routine communication to keep the spark alive.

Effective communication is the cornerstone of a flourishing long distance relationship. It helps overcome the challenges posed by distance, builds trust and understanding, and nurtures a deep emotional connection. By mastering the art of long distance conversations, you can create a strong foundation for your relationship and navigate the complexities of love across miles.

The Power of Communication: Mastering the Art of Long Distance Conversations

Learning how to overcome communication barriers and limitations imposed by distance is essential to maintaining a strong and fulfilling long distance relationship. In this section, we will explore common barriers that can hinder effective communication in long distance relationships and provide strategies to help you overcome them.

One of the most obvious barriers to communication in a long distance relationship is the difference in time zones. When you and your partner are in different time zones, finding a suitable time to connect can be challenging. However, by establishing a regular schedule for check-ins and being flexible with your availability, you can ensure that you have dedicated time to communicate with each other. Setting a routine for communication will not only help you stay connected but also create a sense of stability and predictability in your relationship.

Cultural differences can also present communication challenges in a long distance relationship. Each culture has its own unique communication styles and norms, and understanding and respecting these differences is crucial. Take the time to learn about your partner's culture, language, and customs. This will not only deepen your understanding of each other but also enable you to navigate potential misunderstandings or miscommunications more effectively.

Language barriers may also arise in long distance relationships, especially if you and your partner speak different languages. While it may seem daunting at first, learning some basic phrases or enrolling in language classes can make a significant difference in your ability to communicate. Even if you're not fluent, making an effort to speak your partner's language shows that you value their culture and are willing to bridge the communication gap.

In addition to these barriers, technology can sometimes pose limitations on communication. Poor internet connection, dropped calls, or technical glitches can disrupt your conversations. However, there are ways to overcome these obstacles. Utilize various communication platforms and apps that are reliable and convenient for both of you. Experiment with different options such as video chats, voice messages, or even old-fashioned letter writing to maintain a sense of connection. Remember that technology should be used as a tool to enhance your communication, not replace it entirely.

To foster effective communication in a long distance relationship, it's important to establish healthy communication habits. This includes scheduling regular check-ins and sticking to them, regardless of the physical distance. Use shared calendars or online tools to coordinate your schedules and plan virtual dates or activities together. These small gestures can help create a sense of togetherness even when you're miles apart.

Another crucial aspect of overcoming communication barriers is being open and receptive to your partner's needs and concerns.

Actively listen to what they have to say, show empathy, and validate their feelings. When conflicts arise, approach them with an open mind and a willingness to understand each other's perspectives. Effective communication involves expressing your own feelings, desires, and concerns while also being receptive to your partner's.

By implementing these strategies, you can overcome the communication barriers that distance may impose on your relationship. Remember that effective communication requires effort, patience, and a genuine desire to stay connected. With practice and dedication, you can master the art of long distance conversations and create a strong foundation for your relationship.

The Power of Active Listening: Strengthening Connection and Understanding

In a long distance relationship, where physical proximity is often absent, effective communication becomes even more crucial. It is through communication that you can bridge the distance, maintain a sense of connection, and nurture emotional intimacy with your partner. One key aspect of communication that plays a significant role in building a strong foundation for your long distance relationship is active listening.

Active listening goes beyond simply hearing the words your partner is saying. It involves fully engaging with their thoughts and emotions, demonstrating genuine interest, and striving to understand their perspective. By actively listening, you create space for empathy, validation, and meaningful connection. In this section, we will explore the importance of active listening and provide you with practical tips and techniques to enhance your active listening skills.

Why is active listening important in maintaining a strong connection with your partner? When you actively listen, you show your partner that their thoughts, feelings, and opinions are valued. This fosters a sense of trust and validation, making them more likely to open up and share their innermost thoughts and emotions. By actively listening, you also gain a deeper understanding of your partner's needs and desires, which can help you navigate challenges and conflicts more effectively.

To improve your active listening skills, consider implementing the following techniques:

1. Ask open-ended questions: Instead of asking yes or no questions, encourage your partner to elaborate by asking questions that require more thought and reflection. For example, instead of asking, "Did you have a good day?", ask, "What was the highlight of your day?"

2. Paraphrase and summarize: After your partner expresses themselves, paraphrase their main points to ensure you understood them correctly. Summarize the key takeaways of the conversation to demonstrate your attentiveness and show that you value what they shared.

3. Maintain eye contact: If you're engaging in a video call or meeting your partner in person, maintain eye contact to convey your undivided attention. This non-verbal cue can make your partner feel heard and understood.

4. Practice empathy: Put yourself in your partner's shoes and try to understand their emotions and experiences. Validate their feelings by acknowledging and affirming them. For example, you can say, "It sounds like you're feeling really frustrated right now. I understand why that would be difficult for you."

By incorporating these techniques into your communication routine, you can significantly enhance your active listening skills and foster a deeper emotional connection with your partner.

In addition to active listening, empathy and validation play vital roles in effective communication. Empathy involves understanding and sharing the feelings of another person, while validation acknowledges and validates their emotions and experiences. When you express empathy and validation, you create a safe and supportive space for your partner to express themselves authentically.

To cultivate empathy and validation in your long distance relationship, consider the following tips:

1. Be present and attentive: Show genuine interest in your partner's thoughts and emotions. Put aside distractions and actively engage with what they are saying.

2. Reflect on your partner's perspective: Imagine how you would feel in their situation and try to understand their emotions from their point of view. This empathy allows you to connect on a deeper level.

3. Validate their feelings: Acknowledge and validate your partner's emotions, even if you may not fully understand or agree with them. Let them know that their feelings are valid and that you are there to support them.

By incorporating these practices into your conversations, you can create a space where both you and your partner feel understood, supported, and emotionally connected.

Remember, active listening, empathy, and validation are essential ingredients for effective communication in a long distance relationship. By mastering these skills, you can overcome the barriers imposed by distance, strengthen your connection, and lay the foundation for a thriving long distance love story.

Exploring different forms of communication (e.g., phone calls, video chats, text messaging) and their pros and cons:

Communication is the lifeline of any relationship, and in a long distance relationship, it becomes even more crucial. While physical distance may separate you and your partner, technology has provided us with various means to bridge that gap. In this section, we will explore different forms of communication and discuss their pros and cons, helping you find the best way to connect with your loved one.

Phone Calls:
Phone calls have been a staple of long distance communication for years. They offer real-time interaction, allowing you to hear the tone of voice and express emotions more effectively. Whether it's a quick catch-up or an in-depth conversation, phone calls can provide a sense of closeness. However, availability and cost can be limitations, especially if you are in different time zones or have varying schedules.

Video Chats:
Video chats have revolutionized long distance communication by allowing face-to-face conversations. They offer a more intimate experience, enabling you to see each other's expressions and body language. Video chats can help foster a stronger connection and reduce feelings of loneliness. However, they require a stable internet connection and can be affected by time zone differences or technical glitches, causing frustration at times.

Text Messaging:
Text messaging offers a convenient way to stay connected throughout the day, no matter where you are. It allows for quick exchanges, sharing of photos or videos, and sending cute little messages to brighten each other's day. Texting provides flexibility and can be easily integrated into busy schedules. However, it lacks the depth of verbal or visual communication and can sometimes lead to misinterpretations due to the absence of non-verbal cues.

Other Forms of Communication:
Apart from the traditional modes of communication, there are numerous other options available to couples in long distance relationships. Social media platforms, email, and instant messaging apps offer additional channels for staying connected.

These platforms provide a space for sharing moments, thoughts, and even planning surprise visits. However, it's important to note that not all forms of communication may be suitable for everyone. It is essential to find the ones that work best for you and your partner.

Recommendations for utilizing different forms of communication based on specific situations or preferences:
Every couple is unique, and what works for others may not work for you. It's important to consider your specific situations and preferences when deciding which forms of communication to utilize.

Here are some recommendations to help you navigate through the various options:

- If you value real-time interaction and want to hear each other's voices, prioritize phone calls or video chats. Set regular times for these conversations to establish a routine.

- If you enjoy sharing everyday moments and want to stay connected throughout the day, text messaging or social media platforms can be your go-to. Keep in mind that finding a balance between texting and other forms of communication is crucial for maintaining a healthy level of intimacy.

- When distance and time zone differences make synchronous communication challenging, consider asynchronous methods like email or voice messages. These allow you to share longer updates or express your feelings without the pressure of immediate response.

Remember, the key is to have open communication with your partner about your preferences and find a balance that works for both of you. Experiment with different forms of communication and adapt as needed. The goal is to find ways to maintain your connection, share your lives, and feel close despite the physical distance.

In the next sections, we will delve deeper into the art of mastering effective communication in a long distance relationship. We will explore strategies to overcome communication barriers, develop active listening skills, and foster open and honest conversations. By the end of this chapter, you will be equipped with the tools to communicate effectively and strengthen the bond with your partner, no matter how many miles separate you.

The Power of Consistent Communication: Nurturing Connection in a Long Distance Relationship

Maintaining consistent and regular communication with your partner is the key to nurturing connection and intimacy in a long distance relationship. In this chapter, we will explore the importance of setting communication routines and expectations, provide tips for scheduling regular check-ins despite time zone differences or busy schedules, discuss the benefits of shared calendars or online tools for coordination and communication, and offer suggestions for adding excitement to routine communication.

Setting communication routines and expectations is vital in a long distance relationship. By establishing a consistent schedule for check-ins, you create a sense of stability and reliability for both you and your partner. It allows you to look forward to these dedicated times of connection and reduces uncertainty about when you will hear from each other. Discuss your preferred communication methods and frequency with your partner, taking into account your respective schedules and time zones. This open conversation will help you find a balance that works for both of you.

Despite the challenges posed by time zone differences or busy schedules, it is crucial to maintain regular contact. Make an effort to find overlapping time slots where you can have meaningful conversations, whether it's early morning or late at night. If your schedules don't align easily, consider sacrificing a bit of sleep or adjusting your routines to accommodate quality time together. Flexibility and compromise are essential in keeping the lines of communication open.

Shared calendars or online tools can be invaluable resources for coordinating and enhancing communication in a long distance relationship. Use platforms like Google Calendar or shared to-do lists to keep track of each other's schedules, important dates, and upcoming events. This not only helps in planning virtual dates or surprise messages but also ensures that you are aware of each other's commitments and availability. Having a visual representation of both your lives can foster a sense of togetherness, even when physically apart.

Spicing up routine communication is essential to keep the spark alive in your long distance relationship. Surprise messages are a simple yet effective way to show your partner that you're thinking of them. Send a heartfelt text, voice message, or even a handwritten letter to brighten their day. Additionally, plan virtual dates where you can enjoy activities together from a distance. Watch a movie simultaneously while video chatting, have a virtual cooking date, or play online games together. These creative and interactive experiences will help create shared memories and deepen your bond.

Remember, consistent and regular communication is the lifeline of any long distance relationship. By setting communication routines and expectations, utilizing shared calendars or online tools, and injecting excitement into routine communication, you can maintain a strong connection with your partner despite the physical distance. Stay dedicated to fostering open and honest communication, as it is the foundation for trust, understanding, and emotional intimacy in your long distance love story.

Recognizing the significance of open and honest communication in building trust and intimacy in a long distance relationship:

In a long distance relationship, open and honest communication serves as the foundation for trust, understanding, and emotional connection. We understand that expressing your feelings, concerns, and desires can be challenging when you are miles apart from your partner. However, it is crucial to recognize the significance of transparency and openness in creating a strong and fulfilling long distance relationship.

Transparency and openness play a vital role in fostering trust and emotional connection. When you communicate openly with your partner, you demonstrate your willingness to share your thoughts and emotions, creating an environment of trust and vulnerability. By expressing your feelings, concerns, and desires, you allow your partner to understand you on a deeper level, leading to a stronger emotional bond.

Navigating difficult conversations is an essential skill in any relationship, and it becomes even more critical in a long distance setting. We acknowledge that conflicts and disagreements are inevitable, but they should not be avoided. Instead, learn how to address them effectively and respectfully. When conflicts arise, it is important to approach them with empathy and understanding, keeping in mind that your partner's perspective may differ from yours. By actively listening to their point of view and expressing your own in a respectful manner, you can work towards finding a resolution that strengthens your relationship.

Expressing your needs and desires is equally important in a long distance relationship. We advise you to communicate your expectations and boundaries openly, as it allows your partner to understand your needs and support you. By expressing yourself honestly, you create an opportunity for your partner to reciprocate and meet your needs. Remember, effective communication is a two-way street, and both partners should feel comfortable expressing their thoughts and desires without fear of judgment.

Using "I" statements instead of "you" statements can help avoid blaming or accusing your partner, fostering a more constructive dialogue. We emphasize the importance of active listening during these conversations, ensuring that you understand and validate your partner's emotions and concerns.

We encourage you to celebrate the joys and successes in your long distance relationship. Sharing positive experiences and expressing appreciation for your partner's efforts can boost morale and create a sense of closeness, even when physical distance separates you. By maintaining a positive and supportive communication style, you can strengthen your emotional connection and build a solid foundation of trust and intimacy.

Remember, effective communication requires effort and practice, but the rewards are immeasurable. By recognizing the significance of open and honest communication in building trust and intimacy, you can nurture a strong and fulfilling long distance relationship. We are here to guide you through the challenges and provide practical advice to help you master the art of long distance conversations.

CHAPTER 2: NURTURING TRUST: BUILDING A STRONG FOUNDATION FOR A LONG DISTANCE RELATIONSHIP

Open and Honest Communication: The Key to Trust

In any relationship, communication is vital, but in a long distance relationship, it becomes even more crucial. When you're physically apart from your partner, open and honest communication is the foundation upon which trust is built. By sharing your feelings, concerns, and expectations openly, you create a safe and secure space for both of you to express yourselves freely.

It's essential to schedule regular check-ins with your partner to ensure that you stay connected despite the distance. Set aside dedicated time for video calls or phone conversations where you can truly focus on each other. Utilize technology to its fullest potential by sending voice messages throughout the day or having virtual dates that allow you to share experiences together, even from afar.

However, it's important to acknowledge that communication barriers may exist in a long distance relationship. Language differences or varying time zones can pose challenges, but they should never be insurmountable obstacles. Find ways to overcome these barriers by learning each other's language, using translation tools, or finding suitable times to connect that work for both of you. It may take some effort, but the rewards of effective communication are immeasurable.

Consistency and Reliability: Building Trust Brick by Brick

Trust is not an overnight achievement; it is built over time through consistent actions and reliable behavior. In a long distance relationship, it becomes even more critical to demonstrate your trustworthiness. One way to do this is by keeping your promises and commitments.

When you make a promise, whether it's planning a visit or being available for a scheduled call, follow through on it. Consistency and reliability create a strong sense of security and reliability in your partner's mind. By being accountable and dependable, you show them that they can rely on you no matter the distance.

Sharing Vulnerability: Deepening Emotional Connection

In a long distance relationship, vulnerability plays a significant role in building trust and deepening emotional connection. It's important to create a safe space where both you and your partner can share your emotions openly. This means expressing your feelings, fears, and insecurities without fear of judgment or rejection.

To effectively share vulnerability, practice active listening and empathy. Truly listen to what your partner has to say, validate their emotions, and respond with understanding and support.

Use techniques like repeating back what they've said or asking clarifying questions to ensure that you fully understand their perspective. By creating an environment of emotional safety, you foster trust and intimacy in your long distance relationship.

Active Listening: The Bridge to Trust

Active listening is a powerful tool in nurturing trust. It involves giving your partner your undivided attention, focusing on their words, and responding with genuine interest. When your partner expresses concerns, fears, or insecurities, listen attentively without judgment or invalidation.

Improving your listening skills takes practice. Make a conscious effort to avoid distractions during conversations, such as checking your phone or watching television. Show genuine interest in what your partner is saying by asking follow-up questions and seeking clarification when needed. By actively listening, you demonstrate your commitment to understanding your partner's perspective and building trust in your long distance relationship.

Transparency and Trustworthiness: Balancing Privacy and Openness

Transparency plays a vital role in establishing trust in a long distance relationship. Being open and honest about your daily activities, social interactions, and personal boundaries helps your partner feel secure and included in your life, despite the physical distance.

However, it's also essential to maintain privacy and respect personal boundaries. Find a balance between sharing information and maintaining individuality. Discuss your comfort levels and establish guidelines for what information is appropriate to share. By finding this balance, you can foster trust without sacrificing personal privacy.

In the next sections of this chapter, we will explore more ways to nurture trust in a long distance relationship.

By understanding the importance of open communication, consistency, vulnerability, active listening, transparency, and trustworthiness, you are well on your way to building a strong foundation for your relationship. Trust takes time to develop, but with dedication and effort, you can create a bond that withstands any distance.

Consistency and Reliability: Building Trust through Promises and Commitments

Building trust is essential for any relationship, but it becomes even more crucial in a long distance relationship where physical proximity is limited. Trust forms the foundation on which you and your partner can build a strong and lasting connection despite the distance. One of the key ways to nurture trust is by consistently following through on promises and commitments.

When you make a promise or commitment to your partner, whether it's as simple as calling at a specific time or as significant as planning a future visit, it's important to prioritize it and ensure that you fulfill it. By doing so, you demonstrate not only your reliability but also your dedication to your partner and the relationship as a whole.

Consistency and reliability go hand in hand when it comes to building trust. Consistency means being predictable in your actions and behavior, while reliability refers to your ability to be counted on. When your partner sees that you consistently keep your promises and commitments, they begin to feel secure in the knowledge that they can rely on you. This reliability creates a sense of stability and strengthens the bond between you, making it easier to weather the challenges of distance.

Let's consider an example to illustrate how consistency and reliability can build trust over time. Imagine you and your partner have made a pact to have a virtual date night every Saturday evening, where you both dress up, prepare a special meal, and spend quality time together. Your partner eagerly looks forward to these evenings, knowing that you are committed to making them happen. Even when unexpected circumstances arise, you make it a priority to reschedule rather than canceling outright. Through your consistency and reliability, your partner begins to trust that you value and prioritize their happiness, strengthening the foundation of your relationship.

To stay accountable and reliable in a long distance relationship, consider implementing the following tips:

1. Be realistic with your commitments: It's important to set realistic expectations for yourself and your partner. Avoid making promises that you may struggle to keep or commitments that are beyond your control. By being honest and transparent about your limitations, you can prevent unnecessary disappointment or frustration.

2. Communicate openly about changes: Life is unpredictable, and sometimes unexpected circumstances may arise that prevent you from fulfilling a promise or commitment. When this happens, communicate with your partner as soon as possible. Discuss alternative options or reschedule to show your dedication to meeting your obligations.

3. Prioritize your partner and the relationship: Consistently remind yourself of the importance of your partner and the relationship. Make a conscious effort to prioritize your commitments to your partner over other distractions and responsibilities. By doing so, you demonstrate your commitment and build trust.

4. Practice self-discipline: Long distance relationships require discipline and self-control. Stay committed to your promises and commitments, even when faced with temptations or competing priorities. Remember that trust is built over time through consistent actions.

By consistently keeping your promises and commitments, you

nurture trust and strengthen the foundation of your long distance relationship. Your reliability sends a message to your partner that they can rely on you, even when you're physically apart. In turn, this builds a sense of security, intimacy, and connection between you both. Stay true to your word, and watch as your trust in each other grows stronger with every passing day.

Showing vulnerability and sharing emotions can deepen emotional connection and build trust in a long distance relationship.

In a long distance relationship, showing vulnerability and sharing emotions play a crucial role in establishing a deep emotional connection and building trust between partners. When you open up to your partner and express your true feelings, it creates an environment of authenticity and understanding that strengthens your bond. In this section, we will explore the significance of vulnerability and emotional openness in a long distance relationship, techniques for expressing emotions and vulnerability effectively, and ways to create a safe and supportive space for emotional sharing.

Understanding the significance of vulnerability and emotional openness in a long distance relationship:

Vulnerability is the willingness to expose your inner thoughts, fears, and insecurities. In a long distance relationship, vulnerability allows you and your partner to connect on a deeper level by sharing your emotional experiences and being transparent about your vulnerabilities. By showing vulnerability, you are demonstrating trust and inviting your partner to do the same. This mutual sharing of emotions leads to a stronger emotional connection and a deeper understanding of each other's needs and desires.

Techniques for expressing emotions and vulnerability effectively:

1. Practice active and empathetic listening: When your partner shares their emotions or concerns, give them your undivided attention. Show empathy by validating their feelings and offering support. Reflecting back on what they've shared can show that you genuinely understand and care for their emotions.

2. Use "I" statements to express your own emotions: Begin your sentences with "I feel" or "I am" to express your emotions clearly and directly. This helps avoid accusations or blame, fostering a non-judgmental environment where both partners feel safe to share their feelings.

3. Write heartfelt letters or emails: Take advantage of the written word to express your emotions in a thoughtful and meaningful way. Writing letters or emails allows you to carefully choose your words and express yourself more openly.

Ways to create a safe and supportive space for emotional sharing:

1. Establish clear boundaries: Discuss and agree upon the boundaries of emotional sharing. This can include topics that are off-limits or triggers that may cause discomfort. Respecting each other's boundaries creates a safe space for open communication without fear of judgment or criticism.

2. Practice non-reactive listening: When your partner shares their emotions, avoid immediately reacting or trying to solve the problem. Instead, focus on understanding their perspective and offering empathy and support. Sometimes, all your partner needs is a listening ear.

3. Schedule regular emotional check-ins: Set aside dedicated time to discuss your emotional well-being and any concerns or insecurities you may have. This intentional practice reinforces the importance of emotional connection and provides an opportunity for both partners to openly share their feelings.

By embracing vulnerability and creating a safe space for emotional sharing, you and your partner can deepen your emotional connection and build trust in your long distance relationship. Remember, it takes time and effort from both sides to establish this level of openness, but the rewards are immeasurable. In the next section, we will explore the role of active listening in fostering trust and effective ways to respond to concerns and insecurities without judgment or invalidation.

4. Trust can be nurtured through actively listening to each other's concerns, fears, and insecurities without judgment.

Building trust is a crucial component of any successful relationship, and in a long distance relationship, it becomes even more vital. When you're physically apart from your partner, trust serves as the foundation that holds your love together. Actively listening to each other's concerns, fears, and insecurities without judgment plays a significant role in nurturing trust and strengthening your bond.

So, how can you enhance your listening skills and create a safe space for open communication?

First and foremost, it's important to understand the role of active listening in fostering trust. Active listening involves giving your partner your undivided attention, showing genuine interest, and fully understanding their perspective. By actively listening, you demonstrate that you value their thoughts and feelings, which in turn builds trust and deepens your emotional connection.

To improve your listening skills, try implementing the following tips:

1. Give your undivided attention: When your partner is sharing their concerns or insecurities, make a conscious effort to be fully present. Eliminate distractions, put away your phone, and maintain eye contact. By devoting your full attention to your

partner, you show them that they are a priority in your life.

2. Repeat back and summarize: After your partner has expressed themselves, repeat back what you understood to ensure you've accurately grasped their message. Summarize their points and ask if there's anything else they would like to add. This technique not only demonstrates active listening but also allows for clarification and validation.

3. Ask clarifying questions: When your partner shares their concerns or fears, ask open-ended questions to gain a deeper understanding. Avoid assuming or jumping to conclusions. Instead, seek clarification and encourage them to elaborate. This shows that you genuinely care about their feelings and are willing to invest the time to understand their perspective.

In addition to improving your listening skills, it's essential to respond to your partner's concerns and insecurities without judgment or invalidation. Remember, everyone's emotions and experiences are valid, and it's crucial to create a safe and non-judgmental space for open communication.

Here are some tips on how to respond effectively:

1. Practice empathy and understanding: Put yourself in your partner's shoes and try to understand their perspective. Validate their feelings by acknowledging their emotions and expressing empathy. Let them know that you are there to support them and that their concerns matter to you.

2. Avoid defensiveness: When your partner shares their fears or insecurities, it can be tempting to become defensive. However, defensiveness only hinders open communication and erodes trust. Instead, focus on actively listening and responding calmly and compassionately.

3. Offer reassurance: Reassure your partner that their concerns are valid and that you are committed to working through them together. Provide them with the comfort and support they need to

feel secure in the relationship.

By actively listening to your partner's concerns, fears, and insecurities without judgment, you create a safe and trusting environment for open communication. This fosters a deeper emotional connection and strengthens the foundation of your long distance relationship. Remember, trust is built over time through consistent practice, so be patient and understanding as you navigate this journey together.

Demonstrating trustworthiness by being transparent about daily activities, social interactions, and personal boundaries promotes a sense of security in a long distance relationship.

In a long distance relationship, trust forms the foundation on which your love can thrive and flourish. Without trust, doubts and insecurities can begin to creep in, causing unnecessary strain on the relationship. One powerful way to nurture trust is by being transparent about your daily activities, social interactions, and personal boundaries. By openly sharing this information with your partner, you create a sense of security and demonstrate your trustworthiness. In this section, we will explore the benefits of transparency, provide guidance on what to share, and offer strategies for maintaining privacy while fostering trust.

Transparency is key in establishing trust because it allows both partners to feel informed and involved in each other's lives. When you share information about your daily routines, such as work or school schedules, hobbies, and interests, it helps your partner understand your life and commitments better. This knowledge fosters a deeper connection and reassures your partner that you are reliable and dedicated to the relationship. Transparency also extends to social interactions, where openly discussing friendships, outings, and social events can help alleviate any concerns or insecurities that may arise.

To promote transparency effectively, it is important to find a balance between sharing enough information and respecting each other's privacy. Aim to be open and communicative without overwhelming your partner with unnecessary details. Start by having an open conversation about what type of information is important to each of you. This can include discussing how often you would like to know about each other's daily activities, the level of detail desired, and any specific boundaries or limitations.

Maintaining privacy is equally important when it comes to demonstrating trustworthiness. While sharing information, it's essential to respect each other's personal boundaries and privacy. Remember that trust is built on mutual respect and understanding. Discuss what aspects of your life you both feel comfortable sharing and where you might need more privacy. This could include topics such as personal struggles, friendships, or professional matters. By having open conversations and establishing clear boundaries, you can maintain a healthy balance between transparency and privacy in your long distance relationship.

In some cases, you may encounter situations where you feel the need to hold back certain information due to privacy concerns or personal reasons. It's crucial to communicate these instances with your partner openly and honestly. Let them know your reasoning behind keeping certain details private, but reassure them that it does not affect your commitment or trust in the relationship. Transparency is about being honest and forthright, even if it means acknowledging the need for privacy at times.

Remember, trust is a two-way street. Encourage your partner to also be transparent and share their daily activities, social interactions, and personal boundaries with you. By fostering an environment of openness and trust, you create a safe space for both of you to grow and deepen your connection.

In summary, demonstrating trustworthiness through transparency is essential for building a strong foundation in a long distance relationship. It promotes a sense of security and reassurance, allowing both partners to feel informed and involved in each other's lives. Strive to find a balance between sharing enough information and respecting each other's privacy, and openly discuss any concerns or limitations. By nurturing trust through transparency, you lay the groundwork for a resilient and thriving long distance relationship.

Building trust in a long distance relationship requires addressing and overcoming any previous trust-related issues that may have affected both partners. Trust is the foundation of any successful relationship, and it becomes even more crucial when you are separated by distance. In this section, we will provide guidance on how to confront and resolve past trust issues, as well as offer tips for cultivating empathy and compassion towards each other's insecurities.

Addressing and overcoming previous trust-related issues is a necessary step in building a strong foundation for your long distance relationship. It's important to acknowledge and discuss any lingering fears or doubts that may stem from past experiences. We understand that trust issues can stem from various sources, such as infidelity, betrayal, or unresolved conflicts. To address these issues, we recommend open and honest communication with your partner.

Start by creating a safe and non-judgmental space where both of you can express your concerns and insecurities. Be willing to listen actively to each other's perspectives without interruption or defensiveness. This will allow you to gain a deeper understanding of the underlying causes of the trust issues and help you work towards resolving them together.

It's essential to approach these conversations with empathy and compassion. Remember that your partner's insecurities may be rooted in past experiences that have nothing to do with you. Avoid blaming or shaming each other, as this will only hinder the process of healing and rebuilding trust. Instead, focus on finding solutions and reassurance that will help alleviate each other's concerns.

We also suggest practicing forgiveness and letting go of past grievances. Holding onto past hurts will only create barriers to trust and prevent your relationship from moving forward. Forgiving your partner and yourself for any past mistakes is a crucial step towards rebuilding trust. By acknowledging that people can change and grow, you can create space for a new and healthier foundation of trust to emerge.

Cultivating empathy and compassion towards each other's insecurities is another vital aspect of building trust in a long distance relationship. It's essential to understand that being separated by distance can amplify feelings of insecurity and vulnerability. We encourage you to put yourself in your partner's shoes and try to see the world from their perspective.

Practice active empathy by actively listening to your partner's concerns and fears without judgment or invalidation. Validate their emotions and let them know that their feelings matter to you. By demonstrating empathy and compassion, you create a supportive environment where both partners feel understood and valued.

Additionally, we recommend consistently showing up for your partner and prioritizing their emotional well-being. Reassure them through words and actions that you are committed to their happiness and security. Keep your promises and commitments, as reliability is crucial in building trust.

In conclusion, addressing and overcoming previous trust-related issues requires open communication, empathy, and compassion. By creating a safe space for honest conversations, practicing forgiveness, and cultivating empathy towards each other's insecurities, you can lay a strong foundation of trust in your long distance relationship. Remember, trust takes time to rebuild, so be patient with each other and celebrate the progress you make along the way.

CHAPTER 3: MANAGING JEALOUSY AND INSECURITIES: OVERCOMING DISTANCE-INDUCED DOUBTS

Recognize the source of jealousy and insecurities in long distance relationships, such as fear of being replaced or feelings of inadequacy due to limited physical presence.

In a long distance relationship, it is not uncommon to experience moments of jealousy and insecurities. These emotions can stem from various sources, such as the fear of being replaced or feelings of inadequacy due to the physical distance between you and your partner. It is important to recognize these sources and understand how they can impact your relationship.

The fear of being replaced is a common source of jealousy in long distance relationships. When you are physically apart, it is natural to worry about your partner forming connections with others. Thoughts like, "What if they find someone closer to them?" or "Will they forget about me?" may cross your mind. However, it is essential to remember that trust is the foundation of any successful relationship. Trusting your partner and their commitment to you is crucial in overcoming this fear.

Feelings of inadequacy can also arise due to the limited physical presence in a long distance relationship. Not being able to be physically present for important moments or provide physical affection can lead to feelings of insecurity. You may question whether you are doing enough or if your partner truly values your presence in their life. These feelings are normal, but it is important to remember that your worth is not solely defined by your physical presence. Your emotional support and connection matter just as much, if not more, in a long distance relationship.

Jealousy and insecurities can have a significant psychological and emotional impact on a long distance relationship. They can create tension, misunderstandings, and even lead to arguments. It is crucial to address these emotions openly and honestly with your partner. Ignoring them or letting them fester can further damage the relationship. By recognizing the source of your jealousy and insecurities, you can begin to work towards overcoming them together.

In the upcoming sections of this chapter, we will provide effective communication strategies to openly discuss and address jealousy and insecurities with your partner. Learning how to communicate your concerns in a non-confrontational manner and actively listening to your partner's perspective can help foster understanding and resolution. Additionally, we will explore the importance of trust and transparency in long distance relationships, as well as techniques to provide emotional support and reassurance.

Remember, managing jealousy and insecurities in a long distance relationship is an ongoing process that requires effort from both partners. By acknowledging the sources of these emotions and working together to address them, you can strengthen your bond and build a solid foundation of trust and love, even across the miles.

Learn effective communication strategies to openly discuss and address jealousy and insecurities with your partner

Effective communication is the cornerstone of any successful long distance relationship. When it comes to managing jealousy and insecurities, open and honest communication is even more crucial. By developing strong communication skills, you can create a safe space for discussing your concerns and finding solutions together. In this section, we will explore various techniques to help you communicate effectively with your partner about jealousy and insecurities.

First and foremost, it is important to understand the significance of open and honest communication as a tool for managing these challenges. By expressing your feelings and concerns openly, you allow your partner to better understand your perspective and provide the support you need. Avoiding difficult conversations or suppressing your emotions may only lead to further misunderstandings and resentment. Remember, your partner is not a mind reader, so it is essential to voice your concerns and fears.

One technique to enhance your communication skills is developing active listening skills and empathy for your partner's concerns. When discussing jealousy and insecurities, try to listen attentively without interrupting. Show genuine interest in understanding their perspective and validate their feelings. Empathy plays a crucial role in fostering understanding and connection, as it allows you to see things from your partner's point of view. By actively listening and demonstrating empathy, you can lay the foundation for a productive conversation.

Initiating conversations about jealousy and insecurities can

THE LONG DISTANCE RELATIONSHIPS GUIDEBOOK

be challenging, as these topics can be sensitive and emotionally charged. To approach these conversations in a non-confrontational manner, it is important to choose an appropriate time and setting. Find a time when both you and your partner are relaxed and have adequate time to discuss without distractions. Begin the conversation by expressing your love and commitment, emphasizing that your intention is to improve your relationship rather than placing blame. Use "I" statements to express your feelings and avoid accusatory language.

To further enhance your communication skills, let's explore some examples of effective communication strategies that promote understanding and resolution. One strategy is the use of "I" statements, which focus on expressing your emotions and needs rather than criticizing or blaming your partner. For example, instead of saying, "You never prioritize our relationship," rephrase it as, "I feel neglected when I don't receive enough quality time with you." This approach encourages your partner to empathize and respond constructively.

Another effective strategy is active problem-solving. After discussing your concerns, work collaboratively with your partner to find solutions and compromises. Brainstorm ideas together and be open to exploring different perspectives. Remember, the goal is not to win an argument but to find common ground and strengthen your relationship. By actively engaging in problem-solving, you demonstrate your commitment to addressing the issues at hand.

Learning effective communication strategies is essential for openly discussing and addressing jealousy and insecurities in your long distance relationship. By emphasizing the importance of open and honest communication, developing active listening skills and empathy, initiating conversations in a non-confrontational manner, and using effective communication strategies, you can promote understanding and resolution. These techniques will foster a stronger connection between you and your partner as you navigate the challenges of distance together.

Developing trust and mutual understanding is crucial in overcoming jealousy and insecurities in a long distance relationship. By being transparent about your daily activities and social interactions, you can create a sense of visibility and reliability that strengthens the foundation of trust between you and your partner.

Transparency in daily activities and social interactions contributes to building trust by reducing uncertainty and increasing feelings of security. When you share your schedules and plans with your partner, it creates a sense of involvement and inclusion, allowing them to feel more connected to your life even from a distance. This transparency also helps establish a sense of reliability, as it shows that you are open and honest about your commitments and priorities.

To share your schedules and plans effectively, you can use various tools and technologies available today. Utilize shared calendars or scheduling apps to keep each other informed about your daily activities. This not only helps in coordinating your communication times but also allows your partner to have a clear picture of your day-to-day life. Additionally, consider sharing photos or updates on your social media platforms to give your partner glimpses into your social interactions and experiences. However, it is important to strike a balance between sharing and oversharing to maintain a healthy level of privacy and individuality.

Reassuring your partner's commitment and loyalty is another important aspect of building trust in a long distance relationship. Consistent words and actions play a vital role in reaffirming your dedication to the relationship. Communicate openly about your feelings and intentions, expressing your love and commitment regularly. Little gestures, such as sending thoughtful messages or surprises, can go a long way in reassuring your partner of your

THE LONG DISTANCE RELATIONSHIPS GUIDEBOOK

loyalty.

In situations where trust issues arise, it is essential to address and resolve them promptly. Open and honest communication is key here as well. Encourage your partner to express their concerns and listen actively to their perspective without becoming defensive. It is important to validate their emotions and work together to find solutions. This may involve setting boundaries, establishing clear expectations, or even seeking professional help if needed.

Remember, trust is built over time through consistent actions and open communication. Be patient and understanding with each other as you navigate the challenges of a long distance relationship. By being transparent about your daily activities and social interactions, and ensuring reassurance of commitment and loyalty, you can strengthen the bond between you and your partner, fostering mutual understanding and trust.

Prioritize Emotional Support and Reassurance: Utilizing Frequent and Meaningful Conversations to Provide Comfort and Alleviate Insecurities

In a long distance relationship, emotional support plays a vital role in alleviating the feelings of jealousy and insecurities that may arise. When you and your partner are physically apart, it becomes even more important to prioritize regular and meaningful conversations to maintain a strong emotional connection. By expressing love, appreciation, and reassurance, you can provide comfort and understanding during times of heightened insecurities.

Understanding the Significance of Emotional Support in Alleviating Jealousy and Insecurities

Emotional support serves as a strong foundation in any relationship, but it becomes particularly crucial in long distance relationships. When physical touch and presence are limited, emotional support acts as a pillar of strength, helping to bridge the gap between you and your partner. By actively participating in each other's lives through frequent and meaningful conversations, you can create a sense of closeness and security that alleviates jealousy and insecurities.

Recommendations for Frequent and Meaningful Conversations to Maintain Emotional Connection

To maintain a strong emotional connection, it is essential to prioritize frequent and meaningful conversations with your partner. Set aside dedicated time to talk, whether it's through phone calls, video chats, or even sending voice messages. Make an effort to be fully present during these conversations, listening attentively and engaging in open and honest communication. By actively investing in your conversations, you can deepen your emotional bond and create a safe space to address any insecurities that may arise.

Tips for Expressing Love, Appreciation, and Reassurance to Your Partner

During a long distance relationship, expressing love, appreciation, and reassurance becomes even more important to combat jealousy and insecurities. Take the time to regularly remind your partner of your feelings for them. Simple gestures such as sending thoughtful messages, surprising them with virtual date nights, or even writing love letters can go a long way in making your partner feel valued and cherished. These expressions of love not only provide comfort but also reinforce the strength of your emotional connection.

Techniques to Provide Comfort and Understanding During Times of Heightened Insecurities

There may be moments when you or your partner experience heightened insecurities due to the distance. During these times, it is crucial to provide comfort and understanding. Actively listen to their concerns, validate their feelings, and offer reassurance. Avoid dismissing their insecurities or becoming defensive. Instead, communicate your understanding and empathy, reminding them that you are committed to working through any challenges together. By offering comfort and understanding, you create a safe space for vulnerability and growth within your relationship.

Remember, emotional support is a powerful tool in overcoming jealousy and insecurities in a long distance relationship. By prioritizing frequent and meaningful conversations, expressing love and appreciation, and providing comfort and understanding during times of heightened insecurities, you can strengthen your emotional connection and navigate the challenges of distance with resilience and grace.

Cultivate Individual Hobbies and Interests: Sustaining Personal Fulfillment in a Long Distance Relationship

In a long distance relationship, it can be easy to become consumed by thoughts of your partner and the longing for their physical presence. While it's natural to prioritize your relationship, it's equally important to maintain a sense of self and personal fulfillment outside of the relationship. Cultivating individual hobbies and interests not only allows you to explore new passions but also reduces dependency on the relationship for validation.

Importance of Maintaining a Sense of Self

When in a long distance relationship, it's vital to remember that you are an individual with your own dreams, aspirations, and interests. By nurturing your personal identity, you create a strong foundation for personal growth and self-worth. This sense of self not only benefits you but also enriches the relationship by bringing new experiences and perspectives to share with your partner.

Suggestions for Exploring New Hobbies and Interests

To cultivate your individuality, it's essential to explore new hobbies and interests that align with your passions. Take this opportunity to delve into activities that you've always wanted to try or rediscover old hobbies that you may have put aside. Whether it's painting, playing a musical instrument, joining a sports team, or volunteering for a cause you care about, pursuing these interests will bring joy and fulfillment into your life.

Balancing Time for Individual Pursuits and Couple Activities

While it's important to dedicate time to individual pursuits, it's equally crucial to find a balance between your personal interests and the need for couple activities and shared experiences. Communicate openly with your partner about your desires and schedule regular quality time together. By finding this balance, you can foster personal growth while continuing to build a strong and connected relationship.

Insight into Reducing Dependency on the Relationship for Validation

Cultivating individual identities helps reduce dependency on the relationship for validation. When you have your own interests and accomplishments, you rely less on your partner's validation for a sense of worth. By focusing on personal growth and fulfillment, you develop a stronger self-esteem and confidence that enhances your overall well-being. This newfound resilience and inner strength will not only benefit you but also positively impact your relationship, allowing you to support each other in healthier and more fulfilling ways.

Remember, maintaining a sense of self doesn't mean neglecting your relationship. It means recognizing the importance of personal growth and fulfillment as pillars of a successful long distance relationship. Embrace the opportunity to explore new hobbies and interests, find the right balance between individual pursuits and couple activities, and reduce dependency on the relationship for validation. By doing so, you'll not only strengthen your sense of self but also contribute to the overall health and happiness of your long distance love story.

Managing Jealousy and Insecurities: Seek Professional Help to Deepen Your Understanding and Strengthen Your Relationship

Many long distance relationships are plagued by feelings of jealousy and insecurities. The physical distance can amplify these emotions, leaving you questioning your partner's loyalty or feeling inadequate due to the limited time you spend together. While open communication and trust-building techniques can go a long way in addressing these challenges, there may be times when seeking professional help becomes necessary to navigate deeper underlying issues.

When should you consider seeking professional help? If you find that your feelings of jealousy and insecurities are persistent and causing significant distress in your relationship, it may be time to reach out for guidance. A trained therapist can provide valuable insights and strategies to better understand the root causes of these emotions, helping you develop healthier coping mechanisms and patterns of thinking.

There are different therapeutic options available to couples in long distance relationships. Couples therapy, also known as relationship counseling, allows you and your partner to work through your challenges together with the guidance of a qualified therapist. This form of therapy focuses on improving communication, fostering intimacy, and resolving conflicts in a healthy and productive manner. By engaging in couples therapy, you can gain a deeper understanding of each other's needs and learn effective strategies to manage jealousy and insecurities.

Alternatively, individual counseling can also be beneficial in addressing personal issues that contribute to jealousy and insecurities. In this form of therapy, you have the opportunity to explore your own thoughts, emotions, and behaviors in a safe and supportive environment. Through individual counseling, you can gain insight into your own insecurities, develop self-compassion, and learn coping mechanisms to manage jealousy more effectively.

Seeking professional help can provide numerous benefits for your long distance relationship. A trained therapist can offer an objective perspective and unbiased guidance, creating a space where both you and your partner can freely express your concerns and fears. They can help you identify and address deeper underlying issues that may be contributing to jealousy and insecurities, such as past traumas or unresolved relationship patterns. Additionally, a therapist can equip you with tools and techniques to promote healthy communication, build trust, and strengthen your emotional connection despite the physical distance.

It is important to recognize when seeking professional help becomes necessary. If the feelings of jealousy and insecurities persist despite your best efforts to address them, or if they are causing significant distress or strain in your relationship, reaching out for professional guidance is a proactive step towards finding resolution and achieving a more fulfilling long distance relationship.

In conclusion, seeking professional help through couples therapy or individual counseling can be an invaluable resource in managing jealousy and insecurities in your long distance relationship. Therapists can provide a safe and supportive environment to explore the root causes of these emotions, offer guidance on effective communication and trust-building strategies, and help you navigate deeper underlying issues that may be contributing to your struggles. By taking this step, you are investing in the growth and strength of your long distance love, ensuring a healthier and more fulfilling future together.

CHAPTER 4: HEALTHY BOUNDARIES: BALANCING INDEPENDENCE AND TOGETHERNESS IN LONG DISTANCE LOVE

Understanding individual needs:

In a long distance relationship, it's crucial to recognize that both you and your partner have unique personal boundaries and requirements for independence. Each of you has your own set of needs, desires, and preferences that contribute to your overall well-being and happiness. Understanding and respecting these individual needs is essential for maintaining a healthy and fulfilling long distance relationship.

Respecting and balancing individual needs with the need for emotional togetherness is key. While it's natural to yearn for constant connection and closeness with your partner, it's equally important to honor each other's need for personal space and independence. By acknowledging and respecting these boundaries, you can create a foundation of trust, respect, and understanding in your relationship.

It's important to communicate openly and honestly about your individual needs and expectations. Discussing your boundaries with your partner will help establish clear guidelines and prevent misunderstandings. By expressing your personal preferences, comfort levels, and potential conflicts related to boundaries, you can ensure that both partners' needs are met and understood.

Remember, the goal is not to restrict each other's freedom or limit your experiences. Instead, it's about finding a balance that allows both of you to thrive individually while nurturing your emotional connection. It's about understanding that you can support each other's independence without compromising the strength of your relationship.

In a long distance relationship, there may be challenges in maintaining a sense of togetherness due to physical distance. However, by recognizing and honoring each other's individual needs, you can navigate these challenges with grace and understanding. This means giving each other the space to pursue personal interests, hobbies, and goals without feeling threatened or neglected.

Finding this balance requires open and ongoing communication. Regularly check in with each other to ensure that both of you feel heard, understood, and respected. Reflect on any adjustments that may be necessary to accommodate changing circumstances or personal growth.

Remember, the key to a successful long distance relationship is mutual respect and understanding. By acknowledging and respecting each other's individual needs, you can create a strong foundation that allows your love to flourish across the miles. Embrace the opportunity to nurture your own growth and independence while still fostering a deep emotional connection with your partner.

In the upcoming chapters, we will delve deeper into strategies for navigating boundaries, managing jealousy, and finding ways to stay connected despite the physical distance. With the guidance and insights shared in this book, you will be empowered to strengthen your long distance relationship, ensuring that it thrives and brings fulfillment to both you and your partner.

Open and honest communication: Establishing clear and open lines of communication to discuss and negotiate boundaries within the relationship

Communication lies at the heart of any successful relationship, and long distance love is no exception. In fact, when physical distance separates you from your partner, effective communication becomes even more crucial. It serves as the bridge that connects your hearts, allowing you to navigate the challenges of balancing independence and togetherness.

To establish clear and open lines of communication, start by creating a safe and judgment-free space where both you and your partner can freely express your thoughts, feelings, and concerns. Remember, honesty is key. You must be open and transparent about your personal preferences, comfort levels, and boundaries. This will help both of you understand each other's needs and work towards finding a mutually satisfying balance.

When discussing boundaries, it's important to approach the conversation with empathy and respect. Remember that each person has unique requirements for independence, and it's essential to acknowledge and honor those needs. By listening attentively to your partner's perspective, you can gain a deeper understanding of their boundaries and adjust your own accordingly.

Addressing potential conflicts related to boundaries requires tact and sensitivity. Rather than pointing fingers or placing blame, focus on finding solutions together. Seek common ground and compromise when necessary. The goal is to create a set of boundaries that respects both partners' individuality while nurturing the emotional connection between you.

Effective communication also involves active listening. Pay attention not only to your partner's words but also to their tone of voice, body language, and underlying emotions. By truly hearing and understanding each other, you can avoid misunderstandings and ensure that both partners' needs are met and understood.

When expressing personal preferences and addressing potential conflicts, remember to use "I" statements rather than "you" statements. This helps to avoid sounding accusatory or confrontational. For example, instead of saying, "You always invade my personal space," try saying, "I feel overwhelmed when my personal space is consistently invaded." This approach encourages open dialogue and invites your partner to empathize with your perspective.

Lastly, remember that effective communication goes beyond just talking. It also involves active engagement and attentiveness. Show genuine interest in your partner's thoughts, experiences, and emotions. Ask meaningful questions and provide validation and support. This will foster a deeper sense of connection and strengthen the emotional bond between you, even when miles apart.

By establishing clear and open lines of communication, discussing boundaries, and expressing personal preferences, you lay the foundation for a healthy and balanced long distance relationship. Effective communication ensures that both partners' needs are met and understood, fostering a stronger emotional connection despite the physical distance. So, embrace open and honest communication as a powerful tool to flourish in your long distance love story.

Defining expectations: Open and honest discussions are vital in any relationship, but they become even more crucial in a long distance love affair. When miles separate you from your partner, it's essential to have clarity on what both of you expect in terms of boundaries, alone time, privacy, and shared experiences. By setting clear expectations, you can prevent misunderstandings and future conflicts that may arise due to unmet needs or unspoken desires.

Firstly, take the time to understand your own personal boundaries and requirements for independence. Recognize that you have individual needs that are unique to you, and it's perfectly normal to prioritize them. By acknowledging and respecting your own boundaries, you can better communicate them to your partner and ensure they are honored. Remember, healthy relationships thrive on mutual understanding and compromise.

Now, let's delve into the importance of discussing personal expectations openly and honestly. Schedule a dedicated time to sit down with your partner (via video call or in person) and have a heart-to-heart conversation about your boundaries and desires. This is an opportunity to express your preferences, discuss comfort levels, and address any potential conflicts related to boundaries. Remember, the key to effective communication is active listening and empathy. Make sure to give each other the space to express yourselves without judgment.

During this discussion, be mindful of how your personal beliefs and values may influence your boundaries and expectations. Our upbringing, culture, and past experiences shape our perspective on relationships. It's crucial to be aware of these influences and communicate them to your partner. Understanding where each other is coming from will foster a deeper level of empathy and strengthen your connection.

Additionally, defining expectations also involves discussing alone time, privacy, and shared experiences. How much alone time do you need? What activities do you consider private and off-limits? How do you envision creating shared experiences despite the distance? These are questions that should be openly addressed and agreed upon. Remember, there is no one-size-fits-all answer. Each couple will have different needs and preferences. The key is to find a balance that works for both of you.

Lastly, remember that flexibility and compromise are essential in maintaining healthy boundaries. As circumstances change, such as work schedules or personal commitments, it's important to reassess and adjust your boundaries accordingly. Regular check-ins with each other will ensure that your expectations remain aligned and that both partners' needs are being met.

In conclusion, defining expectations is a crucial aspect of maintaining a healthy and fulfilling long distance relationship. By having open and honest discussions about boundaries, alone time, privacy, and shared experiences, you can prevent misunderstandings and future conflicts. Remember to consider how your personal beliefs and values may influence your expectations, and be willing to be flexible and compromise with your partner. By communicating effectively and finding a balance between independence and togetherness, you can create a solid foundation for your long distance love to flourish.

Flexibility and Compromise: Finding the Balance in Long Distance Love

Maintaining a healthy balance between independence and togetherness is crucial for the success of any long distance relationship. In Chapter 4, we explore the significance of flexibility and compromise in building a strong foundation for your connection. By understanding each other's perspectives and finding compromises that benefit both partners, you can navigate the challenges of physical distance while prioritizing the needs of your relationship.

Flexibility plays a vital role in sustaining a long distance love. It requires a willingness to adapt and adjust to the changing circumstances that distance can bring. Recognize that the dynamics of your relationship may shift over time as work schedules, personal commitments, or even time zones change. By remaining flexible, you can ensure that both partners feel supported and understood.

Understanding and considering each other's perspectives is essential when it comes to adjusting boundaries. Each individual has unique needs and expectations, shaped by their own experiences and circumstances. Take the time to empathize with your partner and truly listen to their thoughts and concerns. By doing so, you can find common ground and create compromises that meet both of your needs.

Finding compromises that benefit both partners is a key aspect of maintaining a balance between independence and togetherness. It is important to remember that compromise does not mean sacrificing your own happiness or values. Instead, it involves finding creative ways to meet each other halfway. For example, if one partner needs more quality time together, while the other requires more personal space, you can establish designated times for shared activities and also respect each other's alone time. This way, both of you can feel fulfilled and valued in the relationship.

In order to find these compromises, effective communication is crucial. Openly express your desires, concerns, and boundaries to your partner, and encourage them to do the same. By having honest conversations, you can avoid misunderstandings and address potential conflicts before they escalate. Remember, healthy compromise requires active engagement from both partners, so be receptive to your partner's needs and be willing to negotiate.

While compromise is vital for maintaining a healthy balance, it is equally important to prioritize the needs of the relationship.

This means considering the impact of your decisions on the overall well-being of your partnership. Sometimes, compromises may involve stepping outside of your comfort zone or letting go of certain expectations. By focusing on the bigger picture, you can strengthen the bond you share with your partner and create a foundation built on trust and understanding.

Throughout your long distance journey, it is crucial to regularly reassess and reflect on the boundaries you have established. As circumstances change, your needs and expectations may also evolve. Set aside time to check-in with each other and openly discuss whether the current boundaries are still meeting both partners' needs. Adjustments may be necessary, and by doing so together, you can ensure that your relationship remains balanced and fulfilling.

By embracing flexibility, understanding each other's perspectives, and seeking compromises that benefit both partners, you can navigate the complexities of long distance love successfully. Remember, it is through these acts of compromise and flexibility that you demonstrate your commitment to the relationship. The journey may be challenging at times, but by working together, you can create a love that transcends any distance.

Maintaining individual hobbies and interests: Nurturing Your Independence and Strengthening Your Connection

Long distance relationships can sometimes feel like a constant struggle to find the right balance between togetherness and independence. When miles separate you from your partner, it's easy to lose sight of your own individuality and become solely focused on the relationship itself. However, it is crucial to remember that maintaining your sense of self is just as important for the health of your partnership as it is for your personal well-being.

In this chapter, we will explore the significance of nurturing your individual hobbies and interests while in a long distance relationship. By encouraging each other to pursue your passions even during times of separation, you not only foster personal growth but also contribute to the overall strength of your bond.

Encouraging each other to pursue individual hobbies and interests has numerous benefits. Firstly, it allows you to maintain a sense of independence, which is essential for your personal growth and fulfillment. It gives you the opportunity to explore your own passions, develop new skills, and discover aspects of yourself that may have been overshadowed by the demands of your relationship. By dedicating time to your interests, you continue to evolve as an individual, which ultimately enriches the connection you share with your partner.

Supporting each other's passions demonstrates a deep level of care and respect. When you encourage your partner to pursue their interests, you show them that you value their individuality and want them to thrive, even when you're physically apart. By actively engaging in conversations about their hobbies, asking questions, and expressing genuine interest, you create a supportive environment where both partners feel heard and understood.

Finding ways to incorporate shared interests while honoring individual needs is another key aspect of maintaining a healthy balance. Look for activities that align with both of your passions and find creative ways to engage in them together, despite the distance. For example, if you both enjoy reading, consider starting a virtual book club where you can discuss your favorite novels and share recommendations. If you're both fitness enthusiasts, challenge each other to complete virtual workouts or participate in online classes together. By combining your shared interests with individual hobbies, you create opportunities for connection and shared experiences while still respecting the need for personal space and growth.

Remember, maintaining your individuality doesn't mean

neglecting your relationship; it means nurturing yourself so that you can bring your best self to the partnership. By encouraging each other's hobbies and passions, you foster independence, respect, and personal growth within your long distance journey. Openly communicating your support and finding ways to incorporate shared interests will help you navigate the complexities of balancing togetherness and independence.

Throughout the rest of this chapter, we will delve deeper into the strategies and techniques you can employ to maintain healthy boundaries in your long distance love. We will guide you in having open discussions about expectations, flexibility, and compromise, ensuring that both partners feel heard, valued, and respected. Let's embark on this journey together as we explore the delicate art of balancing independence and togetherness in long distance relationships.

Regular Check-Ins and Reassessment: Nurturing the Growth of Your Boundaries

In the vast expanse that is a long distance relationship, it is essential to establish boundaries that allow both partners to maintain their independence while fostering emotional togetherness. But how can you ensure that these boundaries continue to meet your needs as circumstances change? This section will guide you through the importance of regular check-ins and reassessment, providing you with techniques and strategies to adjust your boundaries accordingly.

Advising Regular Communication and Reflection

To nurture the growth of healthy boundaries, regular check-ins become the cornerstone of your long distance love story. Schedule dedicated times for open and honest communication with your partner. Use this opportunity to reflect on the established boundaries and evaluate whether they are still effectively meeting both of your needs.

During these check-ins, set aside any distractions and truly focus on each other. Ask yourselves questions such as, "Are our current boundaries allowing us to maintain our independence?" and "Do we feel emotionally connected in our togetherness?" By engaging in this reflective process, you can identify areas where adjustments may be necessary.

The Need for Reassessment as Circumstances Change

As life unfolds, circumstances inevitably shift. Whether it's shifting work schedules, personal commitments, or unexpected opportunities, it is crucial to reassess your boundaries accordingly. Recognize that what worked for you both in the past may not be as effective now. Embrace the fluidity of your relationship and be open to redefining your boundaries as needed.

When reassessing your boundaries, consider how external factors are impacting your day-to-day lives. Are there new time constraints that require you to adjust your schedules? Have your personal needs evolved since you last established your boundaries? By addressing these questions, you can adapt your boundaries to fit the current context of your lives.

Techniques for Checking-In and Strategies to Adjust Boundaries

Checking in with each other doesn't have to be a daunting task. In fact, it can be an opportunity for growth and connection. Here are some techniques and strategies to facilitate your check-ins and navigate the process of adjusting boundaries:

1. Scheduled Check-Ins: Set a recurring date and time for your check-ins. Treat them as non-negotiable moments in your week where you prioritize your relationship. Use this time to openly discuss any concerns, desires, or changes you have noticed regarding your boundaries.

2. Reflective Journaling: Encourage both partners to maintain a reflective journal. Write down thoughts, feelings, and

observations about the established boundaries. This practice enhances self-awareness and provides a platform for constructive conversations during check-ins.

3. Open Dialogue: Create a safe space for open dialogue by actively listening and validating each other's experiences. Share your perspectives and feelings regarding the current state of your boundaries. Remember, healthy communication is key to understanding each other's needs and finding common ground.

4. Flexibility and Compromise: When adjusting boundaries, remember the importance of flexibility and compromise. Be willing to meet each other halfway, taking into account the unique circumstances in both your lives. By working together, you can create boundaries that respect individual needs while fostering emotional togetherness.

By regularly checking-in and reassessing your boundaries, you cultivate a relationship that remains attuned to the ever-changing dynamics of life. Embrace the growth and evolution that comes with long distance love, and approach the process of adjusting boundaries as a shared endeavor. Through effective communication, reflection, and flexibility, you can find the delicate balance between independence and togetherness, allowing your relationship to thrive across the miles.

Remember, "Miles Apart, Hearts Connected" is here to support and guide you on this journey. Turn the page and discover more invaluable insights to help you flourish in your long distance love.

CHAPTER 5: SURVIVING THE DISTANCE: COPING STRATEGIES FOR TIMES OF LONELINESS AND EMOTIONAL DISCONNECTION

Understanding the different types of loneliness in long distance relationships

Loneliness is a common challenge in long distance relationships, and it can manifest in different ways. In this chapter, we will explore two distinct types of loneliness that often arise when you're physically separated from your partner: geographical loneliness and emotional loneliness. By understanding these types of loneliness, you'll be better equipped to identify and address the feelings of longing and sadness that can arise during times of distance.

Geographical loneliness is the longing for physical presence.

When you and your partner are miles apart, you may find yourself missing their touch, their scent, and the simple comfort of being in their presence. This type of loneliness can be particularly challenging because the physical aspects of a relationship play a significant role in our emotional well-being. The absence of physical intimacy and shared experiences can intensify the feelings of longing and create a void that can be hard to fill. It's important to acknowledge and validate these feelings, as they are a natural response to the distance between you and your partner.

On the other hand, emotional loneliness stems from feeling disconnected on an emotional level. Even if you communicate regularly, there may be times when you still feel emotionally distant from your partner. This can happen when you're unable to share and experience daily life together, or when communication becomes routine and lacks depth. Emotional loneliness can lead to a sense of disconnection and even doubts about the strength of your relationship. It's crucial to recognize and address this type of loneliness to maintain a strong emotional bond.

These two types of loneliness often intertwine, contributing to a sense of overall longing and sadness. Geographical loneliness can trigger emotional loneliness, as the absence of physical presence can make it harder to connect emotionally. Similarly, emotional loneliness can intensify geographical loneliness, as the lack of emotional connection can make the physical distance feel even more pronounced. By understanding the interplay between these two types of loneliness, you can develop strategies to cope with them effectively.

In the upcoming sections of this chapter, we will explore various coping strategies to help you bridge the emotional distance and navigate times of loneliness and emotional disconnection. We will delve into effective communication strategies, self-care practices, recognizing signs of emotional disconnection, utilizing technology to foster emotional connection, and implementing coping strategies to overcome these challenges.

Remember, you are not alone in facing these struggles. Many couples in long distance relationships have experienced similar feelings of loneliness and disconnection. Drawing from the experiences of successful long distance couples, we have curated a range of practical and innovative strategies to guide you through these difficult times. By applying the advice and techniques outlined in this chapter, you'll be better equipped to navigate the emotional challenges of your long distance relationship and foster a deeper connection despite the physical distance.

Stay tuned for the next sections where we'll dive deeper into these coping strategies and explore how they can transform your long distance relationship.

Developing Effective Communication Strategies to Bridge the Emotional Distance

In a long distance relationship, maintaining emotional intimacy can be a challenge. The physical separation can make you feel emotionally distant from your partner, leading to feelings of loneliness and disconnection. However, there are effective communication strategies that can help bridge the emotional distance and strengthen your bond.

Setting aside dedicated time for deep conversations to maintain emotional intimacy

One of the most crucial aspects of a long distance relationship is creating opportunities for deep and meaningful conversations. It's important to set aside dedicated time where both you and your partner can focus solely on each other without any distractions. This could be a scheduled video call or phone call where you can discuss your feelings, dreams, and aspirations. By actively listening and expressing yourselves honestly, you can nurture emotional intimacy and build a strong connection despite the physical miles between you.

Utilizing video chats to see each other's facial expressions and

non-verbal cues

While text messages and phone calls are great for staying connected, incorporating video chats into your communication routine can significantly enhance the emotional connection. Seeing each other's facial expressions, gestures, and body language can convey emotions that words alone cannot capture. Video chats allow you to feel more present with each other and create a deeper sense of closeness, even when you are physically apart. So, make it a point to schedule regular video calls and enjoy the visual connection that technology provides.

Exploring different communication tools and platforms to enhance connection

In today's digital age, there are numerous communication tools and platforms available that can help you stay connected in unique ways. Experiment with different methods such as voice messages, sending handwritten letters or care packages, or even creating a shared journal where you can write letters to each other. These alternative communication methods can add variety to your interactions and make your conversations more exciting and meaningful. Explore different apps and online platforms that offer features like synchronized movie watching or virtual games, allowing you to engage in shared experiences and create new memories together.

Remember, effective communication is not just about the quantity of communication but also the quality. It's essential to be attentive, empathetic, and present during your conversations. By actively engaging with each other, sharing your thoughts, and listening without judgment, you can bridge the emotional distance and foster a stronger connection. So, make the most of the communication tools available to you and adapt them to fit your unique relationship dynamics.

In the next section, we will delve into self-care practices to cope with loneliness in long distance relationships. Exploring ways to prioritize your mental and emotional well-being will not only help you navigate the challenges of loneliness but also contribute to a healthier and more fulfilling relationship.

CHAPTER 5: SURVIVING THE DISTANCE: COPING STRATEGIES FOR TIMES OF LONELINESS AND EMOTIONAL DISCONNECTION

Exploring self-care practices to cope with loneliness

Loneliness can be one of the most challenging aspects of being in a long distance relationship. The physical distance between you and your partner can lead to feelings of emptiness and longing, which can take a toll on your emotional well-being. However, there are effective coping strategies you can implement to help manage these feelings and thrive in your long distance relationship.

Engaging in hobbies and activities that bring personal fulfillment and create a sense of purpose:

When you're feeling lonely, it's important to focus on yourself and engage in activities that bring you joy and fulfillment. Take this opportunity to explore your passions and interests. Whether it's painting, writing, or playing an instrument, finding activities that you love will not only distract you from the distance but also give you a sense of purpose and accomplishment. By nurturing your own growth and happiness, you'll have more to share with your partner when you do get the chance to connect.

Seeking social support outside of the relationship through friends, family, or support groups:

While your long distance partner may be your primary source of emotional support, it's essential to build a strong support network outside of the relationship as well. Reach out to your friends, family members, or even join online support groups specifically for individuals in long distance relationships. These connections can provide a sense of belonging and understanding, offering you a space to share your experiences and receive empathy and advice from others who are going through similar challenges. Remember, you don't have to face the distance alone.

Prioritizing mental and emotional well-being through practices like mindfulness, self-reflection, and therapy if needed:

Taking care of your mental and emotional well-being is crucial when dealing with the emotions that arise from being physically separated from your partner. Incorporate mindfulness practices into your daily routine, such as meditation or deep breathing exercises, to ground yourself and reduce stress. Self-reflection can also be beneficial, allowing you to gain insights into your emotions and identify any patterns or triggers. Additionally, if you find that your feelings of loneliness and emotional disconnection persist, don't hesitate to seek therapy or counseling. A professional can provide guidance and support as you navigate the challenges of a long distance relationship.

By engaging in activities that bring personal fulfillment, seeking support from others, and prioritizing your mental and emotional well-being, you can effectively cope with loneliness in your long distance relationship. Remember, it's essential to take care of yourself so that you can show up as your best self for your partner. With these self-care practices, you'll be better equipped to navigate the ups and downs of the distance and maintain a strong connection with your loved one.

Next, we will explore how to recognize and address signs of emotional disconnection in your long distance relationship, providing strategies to bridge the gap and foster emotional intimacy.

Recognizing and Addressing Signs of Emotional Disconnection

Emotional disconnection can be a challenging aspect of long distance relationships. When physical distance separates you from your partner, it's essential to remain vigilant and aware of any signs that may indicate a growing emotional gap. By recognizing these signs early on, you can address them proactively and find solutions together, fostering a stronger connection despite the distance.

1. Decreased Engagement in Conversations:
One of the first signs of emotional disconnection is a noticeable decline in engagement during conversations. You may find that neither of you is as invested or present in your interactions as before. Perhaps the conversations have become more superficial, lacking depth or meaningful exchanges. It's important not to dismiss this as a temporary phase or something that will naturally improve over time. Instead, take it as a signal to dig deeper and address the underlying emotional disconnection.

2. Lack of Sharing Personal Experiences:
In a healthy relationship, partners share their daily experiences, triumphs, and challenges with one another. However, when emotional disconnection arises, there may be a decrease in the sharing of personal experiences. You may notice that your partner no longer opens up or actively avoids discussing their emotional state. This lack of vulnerability can further contribute

to emotional distance. Recognizing this pattern is crucial in order to bring back the sense of emotional intimacy that is vital for a thriving long distance relationship.

3. Growing Apathy or Indifference Towards the Relationship:
Apathy or indifference towards the relationship can be an alarming sign of emotional disconnection. You may feel a sense of detachment or notice that your partner has become less invested in the relationship. This may manifest as a lack of enthusiasm or effort put into maintaining the connection. It's important not to ignore these feelings or dismiss them as temporary. Openly communicating about these emotions can help identify the root causes and find ways to rekindle the passion and commitment in your long distance love.

How to Communicate Effectively About Emotional Disconnection and Work Together Towards Solutions

When it comes to addressing emotional disconnection, effective communication is key. Here are some strategies to help you navigate this sensitive topic and work towards finding solutions together:

1. Create a Safe and Judgment-Free Space:
Initiate a conversation with your partner by creating a safe and non-judgmental space where both of you can openly express your feelings. Avoid blaming or accusing each other, as this can escalate tensions. Instead, approach the conversation with empathy and understanding, focusing on your shared desire to strengthen the emotional bond.

2. Use "I" Statements:
During the discussion, use "I" statements to express how you feel without placing blame on your partner. For example, instead of saying, "You never share anything important anymore," try saying, "I've noticed that I miss our deeper conversations and feeling connected through sharing our experiences."

3. Active Listening:
Listen attentively to your partner's concerns and validate their feelings. Show genuine interest in understanding their perspective. Avoid interrupting or becoming defensive. By actively listening, you demonstrate your commitment to resolving the emotional disconnection and rebuilding the connection.

4. Collaborate on Solutions:
Work together to identify potential solutions that address the emotional disconnection. Brainstorm activities or strategies that can bring back the emotional intimacy you once shared. This collaborative approach fosters a sense of teamwork and strengthens the bond between you.

Remember, emotional disconnection is not uncommon in long distance relationships, but it can be overcome with open and honest communication. By recognizing the signs and addressing them proactively, you can bridge the emotional gap and keep your long distance love flourishing. The next section will explore how technology can be harnessed to foster emotional connection and closeness despite the physical distance.

Utilizing technology to foster emotional connection:

In today's digital age, technology has become an invaluable tool for maintaining emotional connection in long distance relationships. By leveraging various communication platforms and tools, you can bridge the physical gap and create a sense of closeness with your partner. This section will explore effective strategies for utilizing technology to foster emotional connection and combat feelings of loneliness and emotional disconnection.

Sending shared memories, such as photos, videos, and voice messages, that evoke positive emotions:
One powerful way to foster emotional connection is by sending

each other shared memories that evoke positive emotions. Take advantage of technology to send heartfelt photos, videos, or voice messages that capture the essence of your relationship. Reflecting on past experiences and reliving cherished moments can evoke feelings of joy and nostalgia, strengthening your emotional bond despite the distance.

Staying updated on each other's daily lives through constant communication:

Constant communication plays a vital role in maintaining emotional connection in a long distance relationship. Make an effort to stay updated on each other's daily lives by sharing even the smallest details. Use messaging apps, emails, or social media platforms to share your thoughts, experiences, and challenges. By being open and transparent about your day-to-day life, you can create a sense of inclusion and involvement in each other's worlds, fostering emotional intimacy even from afar.

Implementing virtual date nights or activities to maintain a sense of shared experiences:

Just because you are physically apart doesn't mean you can't enjoy shared experiences together. Implementing virtual date nights or activities can help recreate the feeling of being together despite the distance. Schedule regular video calls and plan activities that you both enjoy, such as cooking the same meal, watching a movie simultaneously, or playing online games together. Engaging in these shared experiences will give you a sense of togetherness and help strengthen your emotional connection.

Remember, the key to utilizing technology effectively is to prioritize quality over quantity. While constant communication is important, focusing on meaningful interactions that evoke positive emotions is even more crucial. Instead of simply exchanging messages for the sake of it, take the time to engage in deep conversations, share vulnerable thoughts, and actively listen to your partner's feelings.

Additionally, be mindful of the limitations of technology. Despite its benefits, virtual communication cannot fully replace the physical presence and touch that are integral to human connection. It is essential to acknowledge this and find creative ways to bridge the gap. Consider sending care packages with handwritten letters, surprise gifts, or even planning surprise visits when possible. These gestures can go a long way in nurturing emotional connection and reminding your partner of your love and commitment.

By harnessing the power of technology, you can foster emotional connection and combat feelings of loneliness and emotional disconnection in your long distance relationship. Remember to send shared memories that evoke positive emotions, stay updated on each other's daily lives through constant communication, and implement virtual date nights or activities to maintain a sense of shared experiences. Technology can be a powerful tool in bridging the emotional gap and keeping your hearts connected, even when miles apart.

Implementing coping strategies during times of emotional disconnection:

In the vast landscape of long distance relationships, there are bound to be moments when you feel a sense of emotional disconnection from your partner. Whether it's due to the physical distance or the challenges that come with maintaining a strong emotional bond, it's important to have effective coping strategies in place to navigate these difficult times. In this section, we will explore some practical techniques to help you bridge the emotional gap and maintain a fulfilling connection with your loved one.

1. Scheduling regular virtual date nights:
One way to combat emotional disconnection is by creating opportunities for quality time together. Schedule regular virtual

date nights where you can engage in activities or simply have meaningful conversations. This dedicated time allows you to focus on each other, fostering a sense of closeness despite the distance.

2. Practicing empathy and understanding toward one another:
Emotional disconnection can sometimes stem from misunderstandings or miscommunications. It's crucial to approach these situations with empathy and understanding. Put yourself in your partner's shoes and actively listen to their concerns. Validate their feelings and work together to find solutions that address both of your needs.

3. Seeking professional help if necessary to address underlying issues:
If emotional disconnection persists or becomes a recurring issue, it may be beneficial to seek professional help. A licensed therapist can provide guidance and support in navigating the unique challenges of a long distance relationship. They can help you identify underlying issues, develop effective communication strategies, and strengthen your emotional connection.

4. Finding creative ways to bridge the emotional gap:
While technology enables us to stay connected, it's essential to find creative ways to bridge the emotional gap. Surprise gifts or letters sent through mail can evoke joy and excitement, reminding your partner of your love and commitment. Organizing surprise visits, if feasible, can also be a powerful way to rekindle the emotional connection and create lasting memories together.

Remember, coping with emotional disconnection requires effort and commitment from both partners. It's important to continuously communicate, express your needs, and actively work towards reconnecting emotionally. By implementing these coping strategies, you can navigate the challenges of long distance relationships and maintain a strong, fulfilling bond with your loved one.

In the next section, we will dive deeper into utilizing technology to foster emotional connection in long distance relationships. We will explore different ways to leverage technology to enhance communication, maintain intimacy, and feel emotionally connected despite the physical distance. Stay tuned for practical tips and techniques that will help you strengthen your emotional bond even when miles apart.

CHAPTER 6: VIRTUAL CONNECTION: UTILIZING TECHNOLOGY TO CREATE MEANINGFUL INTIMACY ACROSS MILES

Utilize video calls:

Scheduling regular video calls with your partner is essential in maintaining a strong connection and bridging the physical distance between you. Seeing each other's facial expressions and body language can enrich the communication experience and deepen your understanding of one another.

Video calls not only provide visual cues but also create a sense of closeness that cannot be achieved through mere text messages or phone calls. The ability to see your partner's smile, hear their laughter, and witness their reactions in real-time can enhance the emotional connection between you.

To make your video calls more intimate and meaningful, it's important to set the right mood. Find a quiet and comfortable space where you can have uninterrupted conversations. Dim the lights or light candles to create a cozy ambiance. Consider dressing up or wearing something special to make the experience feel more like a date. These small gestures can help recreate the atmosphere of being together physically.

During your video calls, don't hesitate to express your affection verbally. Use words to convey your love, appreciation, and longing for your partner. Hearing those sweet words can make a significant difference in how connected and valued you both feel. Additionally, don't forget the power of physical gestures. Blow kisses, send virtual hugs, or even hold hands against the screen. These actions may seem silly, but they help bridge the gap and remind you both of the physical affection you share.

Remember, the goal of utilizing video calls is to create a meaningful and intimate experience. So, try to engage in deeper conversations rather than just discussing mundane daily events. Ask thought-provoking questions, share your dreams and aspirations, or reminisce about cherished memories. By delving into more meaningful topics, you can foster a stronger bond and keep the conversation engaging and fulfilling.

We understand that maintaining a long-distance relationship can be challenging, but by utilizing technology effectively, you can create an environment that simulates the intimacy of being together physically. Video calls provide a window into each other's lives and allow for emotional connection. By following these tips and techniques, you will be able to make the most out of your video calls and nurture your long-distance love.

Get creative with technology to enhance your long distance relationship. In this section, we will explore various messaging apps, social platforms, and online activities that allow you and

THE LONG DISTANCE RELATIONSHIPS GUIDEBOOK

your partner to engage in shared experiences, fostering a sense of connection and intimacy despite the physical distance.

1. Explore messaging apps and social platforms:
In today's digital age, there are numerous messaging apps and social platforms available that can bridge the gap between you and your partner. Whether it's WhatsApp, Facebook Messenger, or Snapchat, these platforms offer features like video calls, voice messages, and even the ability to send photos and videos instantly. Take the time to explore different apps and find one that suits both of your preferences.

2. Plan virtual date nights:
While being physically apart, you can still enjoy special moments together through virtual date nights. Set a time to cook a meal together while on a video call, creating a shared experience that engages the senses and fosters a feeling of togetherness. Alternatively, choose a movie to watch simultaneously and chat about it afterwards. These activities will not only provide an opportunity for shared experiences but also create lasting memories.

3. Engage in online games:
Online games can be a fun and interactive way to connect with your partner. Choose games that allow you to play together or compete against each other, fostering a sense of friendly competition and shared achievement. Whether it's solving puzzles, playing virtual board games, or even engaging in multiplayer video games, these activities can add an element of excitement and bonding to your relationship.

Remember, the objective is to utilize technology to create meaningful intimacy, so choose activities that align with your shared interests and values. It's important to keep an open mind and be willing to try new things together.

Within the context of this book, we emphasize the importance of exploring these technological options to maintain a strong and fulfilling long distance relationship. By getting creative with technology, you can find innovative ways to connect with your partner, strengthening your emotional bond and creating shared experiences that bridge the physical gap between you.

In the next section, we will delve deeper into the concept of intimate communication through technology, exploring how you can express your emotions and desires openly in a long distance relationship.

Engage in intimate communication:

In a long distance relationship, communication is the lifeline that keeps you connected with your partner. It's not just about exchanging messages or talking on the phone; it's about truly engaging in intimate communication to foster a deeper emotional connection. Through technology, you can express your emotions, desires, dreams, fears, and intimate thoughts, despite the physical distance that separates you.

Using technology platforms, such as texting, voice messages, or even handwritten letters sent electronically, you can create a space for open and honest communication. Take advantage of these tools to express your feelings without hesitation or reservation. Share your hopes and dreams, discuss your fears and insecurities, and let your partner be your confidant. Remember, vulnerability is key in building trust and intimacy, even when you are miles apart.

When engaging in virtual conversations, it's important to be actively present and truly listen to your partner. Avoid distractions and give them your undivided attention. Show genuine interest in what they have to say and ask meaningful questions to delve deeper into their thoughts and emotions. By actively listening and being present during virtual conversations, you can create a sense of closeness and understanding that transcends the physical distance.

Alongside technology, gestures of affection also play a significant role in long distance relationships. Use your words to express your love and admiration for your partner. Tell them how much they mean to you and how grateful you are to have them in your life. Words have the power to bridge the gap between you and your partner, reminding them of your love and commitment.

Additionally, don't underestimate the power of non-verbal communication, even through a screen. Look into each other's eyes during video calls, smile, and indulge in small physical gestures like blowing kisses or sending virtual hugs. These seemingly simple actions can create a sense of physical closeness, reminding you both of the love you share.

Remember, technology is merely a tool to facilitate communication. It's up to you and your partner to utilize it effectively and meaningfully. Embrace the opportunities it presents to express your love, desires, and dreams openly. By engaging in intimate communication, you can deepen your emotional connection and strengthen the bond that holds your long distance relationship together.

In the next section, we will explore the concept of sharing daily routines as a means to stay involved in each other's lives despite the distance.

Share daily routines: Leveraging technology to share the details of your daily lives with each other

In a long distance relationship, it's easy to feel disconnected from your partner's day-to-day life. However, by leveraging technology, you can bridge that gap and foster a feeling of involvement in each other's lives despite the distance. Sharing your daily routines is not only a way to stay connected but also an opportunity to deepen your understanding of each other's experiences and create a sense of shared intimacy.

One way to share your daily routines is by sending pictures of your surroundings. Whether it's a snapshot of a beautiful sunset or a funny moment at work, capturing these moments and sharing them with your partner allows them to visualize and be a part of your daily life. It's a simple gesture that shows you care and want them to be included in your world, even from miles away.

Another way to create a sense of connection is by describing your experiences to each other. Take the time to share the highlights and challenges of your day, whether it's through a text message, voice memo, or even a short video. By opening up about your daily ups and downs, you create an opportunity for your partner to empathize with your joys and offer support during tough times. This level of emotional sharing helps strengthen your bond and fosters a deeper connection.

Virtual meals can also be a great way to share daily routines and create a sense of togetherness. Plan a time when you can both sit down for a meal and have a video call. This allows you to enjoy your favorite dishes while virtually dining together. Not only will this make you feel closer, but it also gives you an opportunity to talk and connect in real-time, just like you would if you were physically sitting across the table from each other. Make it special by cooking the same meal or trying a new recipe together, even if you're in different kitchens.

By sharing your daily routines with each other, you create a space where both partners feel involved and connected. It's not only about the big moments or milestones but also the small, mundane aspects of life that build a strong foundation for your relationship. Through technology, you can stay updated on each other's lives, share joys and challenges, and provide support when needed.

Remember, it's important to approach this sharing with genuine interest and active listening. Take the time to ask questions, show curiosity, and actively engage in conversations about each other's daily routines. This helps your partner feel valued and understood, enhancing the intimacy of your connection.

Sharing daily routines is just one aspect of utilizing technology to create meaningful intimacy across miles. In the following sections of this chapter, we will explore more techniques and strategies to bring you and your partner closer together, making the most out of the virtual world that connects your hearts despite the physical distance.

In a long distance relationship, finding ways to recreate the physical presence of your partner can be a challenge. Fortunately, technology offers numerous opportunities to engage your senses and deepen the connection despite the miles between you. In this chapter, we will explore how incorporating sensory elements can help bridge the gap and make your long distance relationship feel more tangible and intimate.

1. Sharing Music Playlists: Reminders of Shared Memories

Music has a way of evoking emotions and memories like nothing else. By creating and sharing playlists that remind you of special moments or have a significant meaning for both of you, you can transport yourselves back to those cherished times. Whether it's the song that played during your first dance or the tune that always makes you smile, music can bring you closer together even when you're far apart.

2. Cooking Together: A Shared Sensory Experience

Just because you're physically separated doesn't mean you can't enjoy meals together. Set up a video call and plan a cooking session where you both prepare the same dish. As you chop, sauté, and savor the flavors, you'll not only satisfy your taste buds but also create a shared sensory experience. The aroma of food, the sound of sizzling pans, and the enjoyment of a delicious meal will make you feel like you're right there with each other.

3. Setting the Mood: Enhancing Intimacy through Video Calls

Video calls are a lifeline for long distance couples, allowing you to see each other's facial expressions and body language. To make these calls more intimate and meaningful, consider setting the right mood. Dim the lights, light some candles, and create a cozy atmosphere. Express your affection verbally, using tender words and loving gestures. Even through the screen, your partner will feel your warmth and love.

4. Sensory Messaging: Expressing Emotions and Desires

Texting and voice messages have become essential tools for maintaining communication in long distance relationships. Utilize these mediums to express your deepest emotions and desires. Share intimate thoughts, dreams, and fears with each other. You can even try writing handwritten letters and sending them electronically. The act of putting pen to paper adds a personal touch and brings you closer together.

5. Sharing Daily Routines: Involvement in Each Other's Lives

Incorporating sensory elements into your daily routine can help you feel more connected despite the distance. Share pictures of your surroundings, describe your experiences, or even have virtual meals together. By involving each other in your day-to-day lives, you create a sense of presence and involvement that strengthens your bond.

Remember, while technology can facilitate sensory experiences, it's important to actively listen and be fully present during your virtual conversations. Give each other your undivided attention, and cherish the moments you have together.

In the next section, we will explore another way to utilize technology to enhance your long distance relationship: embracing the power of snail mail. Despite living in a digital world, there is still something incredibly special about receiving physical letters or care packages. Let's dive into how you can make snail mail an integral part of your connection and create tangible reminders of your love.

Embrace the Power of Snail Mail: Deepening Your Connection Through Physical Letters and Care Packages

In this digital age, where instant messaging and video calls dominate our long distance relationships, there is something truly special about receiving a physical letter or care package from your partner. Despite living in a world where technology connects us in various ways, the sentimental value of snail mail cannot be underestimated. It adds a tangible element to your connection, reminding you that love knows no boundaries, not even distance.

So, how can you make snail mail more personal and meaningful? Let's explore some ways to create a memorable experience for both you and your partner.

1. Include Personal Touches:
When sending a letter or care package, think about what would make it uniquely yours. Include small tokens of affection, like a handwritten note, a pressed flower from a special place, or a photo of the two of you together. These personal touches will not only show your thoughtfulness but also serve as a physical representation of your love.

2. Surprise with Small Delights:
Snail mail provides an opportunity for surprise and delight. Consider adding small surprises in your letters or care packages, like a favorite candy, a scented candle, or a small trinket that holds meaning for the two of you. These unexpected gestures will bring joy to your partner and ignite a sense of excitement in them.

3. Infuse Favorite Scents:
Our sense of smell has a powerful way of triggering memories and emotions. Consider including a piece of fabric sprayed with your perfume or cologne, a sachet of your partner's preferred scent, or a scented candle that reminds you both of cozy evenings spent together. By infusing familiar scents into your snail mail, you

can strengthen the emotional connection between you and your partner.

4. Create a Tangible Reminder:
The physical nature of snail mail provides a lasting reminder of your love. From handwritten letters to small tokens exchanged, these items can be cherished and revisited whenever you need a reminder of your partner's presence in your life. Keep these treasures in a special box or create a scrapbook filled with your shared memories. By having something tangible to hold onto, you can feel a deeper connection even when you are physically apart.

Remember, the beauty of snail mail lies in its ability to transcend the digital realm and offer a meaningful experience beyond instant communication. While text messages and video calls are essential for staying connected, snail mail adds an extra layer of intimacy and nostalgia to your long distance relationship.

Incorporate the power of snail mail into your routine, whether it's sending handwritten letters, care packages filled with love, or small surprises that make your partner's day. By embracing this traditional form of communication, you can deepen your connection and create a tangible reminder of your enduring love, despite the physical distance.

As you navigate your long distance relationship, keep in mind the importance of finding unique ways to connect beyond the digital world. Snail mail offers a heartfelt and personal avenue to express your love and affection. Embrace this timeless practice, and let it become a cherished part of your long distance love story.

CHAPTER 7: THE POWER OF SURPRISE: INNOVATIVE IDEAS TO KEEP THE SPARK ALIVE IN LONG DISTANCE RELATIONSHIPS

The Power of Surprise: Keeping the Excitement and Spark Alive

In a long distance relationship, it's crucial to maintain a sense of excitement and novelty to keep the spark alive. One way to achieve this is through creative gestures that surprise your partner and show them how much you care. Surprising your partner not only brings joy and happiness but also strengthens the bond between you. The element of surprise can reignite the passion and remind both of you why you are in this long distance relationship.

So, what are some unique and thoughtful gestures you can use to surprise your partner? Let's explore a few examples:

Sending Surprise Care Packages: Delivering a package filled with your partner's favorite things or items that hold sentimental value can instantly brighten their day. It could be a box of their favorite snacks, a handwritten letter, or a small gift that reminds them of your love. The key is to personalize the contents based on their preferences and interests. This thoughtful gesture shows that you are thinking about them even when you're apart.

Arranging Surprise Virtual Experiences: With technology at our fingertips, you can plan surprise virtual experiences for your partner. It could be a surprise video call during their lunch break or arranging a virtual game night with friends. These unexpected moments of connection create lasting memories and help bridge the physical gap between you.

Planning Surprise Visits: Nothing beats the excitement and emotional impact of an unexpected visit. Surprise visits allow you to spend quality time together and make your partner feel truly cherished. Coordinate logistics carefully, keeping the visit a secret until the big reveal. This surprise gesture can strengthen your connection and remind you both of the power of physical closeness.

Maintaining a Sense of Excitement and Novelty

Creative gestures play a vital role in maintaining a sense of excitement and novelty in your long distance relationship. They add that extra spark that keeps the relationship thriving even when you are miles apart. However, it's essential to ensure that these gestures are personalized to your partner's preferences and interests. By tailoring surprises to their unique tastes, you show them that you truly understand and care about their happiness.

Personalization is key when it comes to creative gestures. It shows your thoughtfulness and attention to detail, making your partner feel special and loved. Remember to consider their likes and dislikes, hobbies, and passions when planning surprise gestures. This personal touch will deepen your bond and keep the fire of love burning strong.

In the upcoming chapters, we will explore more ways to keep the spark alive in your long distance relationship. From personalized gifts and unexpected visits to virtual date nights and love letters, we will delve into the various aspects of surprising your partner and nurturing the connection despite the distance. By understanding the power of surprise and incorporating it into your relationship, you can create a strong, fulfilling, and exciting long distance love story. So, let's dive in and discover the innovative ideas that will keep your hearts connected, even when you're miles apart.

The Power of Personalization: Deepening Your Bond through Thoughtful Gifts

In a long distance relationship, it can be challenging to express love and thoughtfulness when physical proximity is not readily available. However, personalized gifts have the power to bridge that gap and serve as a constant reminder of your love and commitment to your partner. By going the extra mile to create something unique and tailored to their preferences, you can deepen the bond between you and keep the spark alive, even across the miles.

Exploring Different Ways to Send Personalized Gifts

When it comes to sending personalized gifts in a long distance relationship, the possibilities are endless. Technology has made it easier than ever to customize and deliver meaningful presents. Consider exploring online platforms that offer personalized jewelry, such as engraved necklaces or bracelets with your initials or a special date. You can also create photo albums filled with cherished memories, capturing the essence of your relationship. Additionally, handwritten letters are a timeless way to personalize your gift, allowing you to pour out your emotions on paper.

The Importance of Showing Love and Thoughtfulness Through

Gift-Giving

Gift-giving is more than just a material exchange; it is a powerful way to show your love and thoughtfulness. In a long distance relationship, where physical touch and proximity may be limited, thoughtful gifts can fill that void and convey your affection. When you take the time to choose or create a gift that reflects your partner's interests, hobbies, or personal preferences, you demonstrate that you truly understand and care for them. This act of thoughtfulness strengthens the emotional connection between you and reminds your partner that they are always on your mind, despite the physical distance.

Examples of Personalized Gifts

Personalized gifts come in many forms, each with its own unique way of touching your partner's heart. For instance, customized jewelry, such as a necklace with their birthstone or a bracelet engraved with a meaningful quote, can be a constant reminder of your love. Photo albums filled with pictures of special moments you've shared together can evoke nostalgia and reinforce the bond you've created. Handwritten letters carry a personal touch that transcends digital communication, allowing you to express your deepest emotions in a tangible way. These examples are just the tip of the iceberg, and the key is to choose gifts that resonate with your partner's preferences and interests.

How Personalized Gifts Deepen the Bond

Personalized gifts hold a special place in the hearts of both the giver and the receiver. By investing time and effort into creating or selecting a personalized gift, you demonstrate your commitment and thoughtfulness. The act of personalization shows that you know your partner on a deep level, understanding their passions, dreams, and desires. This level of understanding fosters a sense of intimacy and strengthens the emotional connection between you. Whenever your partner looks at or uses the personalized gift, they will be reminded of your love and feel a sense of closeness, no matter the physical distance that separates you.

Emphasizing the Impact of Personalization

In a long distance relationship, where physical touch and shared experiences may be limited, personalization becomes even more crucial. It adds a layer of intentionality to your gestures, making them more meaningful and impactful. By creating personalized gifts, you are actively working to deepen the bond between you and your partner, ensuring that they feel cherished and loved. The impact of personalization goes beyond the material value of the gift; it speaks volumes about the effort and care you put into nurturing your relationship, making it an essential ingredient for keeping the spark alive in a long distance relationship.

Remember, the power of personalization lies in its ability to create a lasting impression and strengthen the emotional connection between you and your partner. By choosing or creating thoughtful and personalized gifts, you can keep the flame of love burning, even in the face of distance and separation.

Unexpected visits:
- Planning surprise visits to see your partner and the benefits they offer

When it comes to long distance relationships, surprise visits can be a game-changer. The element of surprise adds a touch of excitement and anticipation that can reignite the spark between you and your partner. These unexpected visits not only provide a much-needed break from the distance but also offer an opportunity to create lasting memories together.

Tips for coordinating unexpected visits (keeping it a secret, considering logistics, etc.)

Coordinating a surprise visit requires careful planning to ensure everything goes smoothly. Here are some tips to help you make the most of your spontaneous rendezvous:

1. Keep it a secret: The element of surprise lies in keeping your visit under wraps until the last moment. Avoid dropping hints or accidentally letting it slip to your partner. This way, when you finally show up at their doorstep unannounced, the impact will be even greater.

2. Consider logistics: Before embarking on your surprise visit, consider practical aspects such as transportation, accommodation, and time off work or school. Take into account any commitments or obligations your partner may have, and choose a time that works best for both of you.

The emotional impact of surprise visits and how they can strengthen the connection

Surprise visits hold immense emotional significance in a long distance relationship. They demonstrate your commitment, dedication, and willingness to go the extra mile to be with your partner. The sheer joy and excitement on their face when they see you standing there unexpectedly can melt away any feelings of distance or loneliness.

These visits also create opportunities for quality time together, allowing you to engage in meaningful conversations, explore new places, and simply enjoy each other's company without the constraints of phone screens and video calls. The emotional intimacy that comes from physical closeness during these visits can strengthen your connection and remind you both why you're willing to endure the challenges of a long distance relationship.

Making the most of the time spent together during the visit

To make the most of your surprise visit, it's important to plan activities that will create lasting memories. Consider exploring local attractions, trying new restaurants, or even embarking on a mini getaway together. These shared experiences will not only deepen your bond but also give you something to cherish and reminisce about when you're apart again.

In addition, don't forget to prioritize quality time alone with your partner. Whether it's a cozy night in, a romantic dinner, or simply taking a walk hand in hand, these moments of intimacy will help you reconnect on a deeper level and reaffirm your love for each other.

Recognition of the value of face-to-face interactions and physical closeness in a long distance relationship

While technology has allowed us to bridge the gap in long distance relationships, there is no substitute for face-to-face interactions and physical closeness. Surprise visits provide an invaluable opportunity to experience these aspects firsthand. Being able to touch, hug, and kiss your partner can reignite the passion and strengthen the emotional connection that distance often challenges.

Remember, surprise visits should be a mutual effort. Communicate with your partner to ensure that they are comfortable with spontaneous visits and that the timing is right for both of you. The element of surprise can be magical, but it's essential to respect each other's boundaries and preferences.

By incorporating surprise visits into your long distance relationship, you'll not only keep the spark alive but also create cherished memories that will sustain you during the periods of separation. The power of unexpected visits lies in their ability to remind you of the joy and love that exists between you and your partner, making the distance seem more bearable and the future together worth fighting for.

Virtual date nights: Creating shared experiences despite the physical distance

In a long distance relationship, finding ways to stay connected and create shared experiences is crucial for keeping the spark alive. Virtual date nights are an innovative solution that allows you and your partner to feel closer, even when you're miles apart. These virtual dates not only provide an opportunity for quality time together but also replicate the feeling of being physically present with each other.

There are various virtual date activities you can explore to enhance your connection. One idea is to cook a meal together. Plan a menu, gather the necessary ingredients, and set up your video call. As you each prepare your respective dishes, you can talk, laugh, and experience the joy of cooking together. Once the meals are ready, sit down and enjoy your virtual dinner date. Sharing a meal, even virtually, creates a sense of intimacy and togetherness.

Another option is playing online games together. Choose a game that you both enjoy and that allows for interaction and friendly competition. Whether it's a virtual game of Scrabble, chess, or even a multiplayer video game, playing together can be a fun and engaging way to bond. You can chat and strategize as you play, making the experience all the more enjoyable.

Watching a movie simultaneously is another virtual date idea that can bring you closer. Pick a movie that you both want to see and synchronize your start times. Set up a video call or use a screen-sharing platform to watch the movie together. You can share your thoughts, reactions, and even pause the movie to discuss certain scenes. This shared movie-watching experience can make you feel like you're cuddled up on the couch together, despite the physical distance.

Virtual date nights offer a way to create shared experiences and maintain a sense of excitement and connection in your long distance relationship. By engaging in activities that you both enjoy, you're able to strengthen your bond and create lasting memories. The regularity and intentionality of these virtual dates are important. Make it a point to schedule them regularly, just as you would with in-person dates. This consistency shows your commitment to keeping the spark alive and demonstrates that your relationship is a priority.

Remember, the key to successful virtual dates is to be present and fully engaged. Treat these virtual experiences as if you were physically together, giving each other your undivided attention. Turn off distractions, focus on the moment, and make the most of the time you have together.

Virtual date nights are just one of the many ways you can keep the excitement alive in your long distance relationship. By exploring innovative ideas and finding creative ways to connect, you'll be able to bridge the physical gap and nurture your love despite the miles between you. So, grab your laptop, plan an engaging virtual date, and let the sparks fly!

The Power of Love Letters and Surprise Notes: Crafting Emotional Connections Across the Miles

In a long distance relationship, where physical touch and face-to-face interactions are limited, finding meaningful ways to connect with your partner becomes crucial. One powerful tool that can bridge the distance and deepen the bond between you and your loved one is the art of written communication. Love letters and surprise notes hold an incredible ability to convey emotions, make your partner feel special, and keep the spark alive in your long distance relationship.

Understanding the impact of written communication is essential. While technology offers instant messaging and video calls, there is something incredibly intimate and personal about a handwritten message. It shows thoughtfulness, effort, and dedication. By taking the time to express your feelings on paper, you create a tangible reminder of your love and commitment for your partner to cherish.

Sending love letters and surprise notes brings forth numerous benefits. Firstly, they provide a sense of anticipation and excitement. Receiving a heartfelt letter or a surprise note in the mail can instantly brighten your partner's day and create a lasting memory. These acts of love act as a reminder of the strength of your connection, even when you're physically apart.

Love letters and surprise notes also allow you to express your emotions freely and openly. In the busyness of life, it can be challenging to find the right moment or the right words to convey how much you care. However, by putting your thoughts into writing, you have the opportunity to share your deepest feelings without interruption or distractions. This level of vulnerability and honesty can bring you closer together, fostering a deep emotional connection.

Wondering what to write in these heartfelt messages? The possibilities are endless, but here are a few ideas to get you started:

1. Express your love and appreciation: Share specific moments when you felt grateful for having your partner in your life. Tell them how much they mean to you and how their presence has positively impacted your life.

2. Recall special memories: Take a trip down memory lane and reminisce about the moments that have shaped your relationship. Remind your partner of the cherished times you've shared together and how they have touched your heart.

3. Share your dreams and aspirations: Paint a vivid picture of your future together. Talk about the goals you want to achieve as a couple and the adventures you long to embark on. By envisioning a shared future, you'll both feel motivated and connected.

4. Compliment and affirm: Highlight your partner's strengths and qualities that you admire. Let them know the specific ways they make you feel loved, supported, and inspired. Your words have the power to lift their spirits and boost their self-confidence.

Remember, regular communication through handwritten messages is vital. Aim to establish a routine where you surprise your partner with love letters or notes regularly. This consistency will build anticipation and excitement, keeping the flame of your relationship alive.

As you write, personalize each letter or note according to your partner's interests and preferences. Show that you truly understand and value them by incorporating inside jokes, shared references, or memories that are unique to your relationship. The more personal and tailored your messages are, the deeper the emotional connection will be.

In conclusion, love letters and surprise notes are potent tools that can transcend the physical distance in a long distance relationship. They allow you to express your emotions authentically, create lasting memories, and foster a strong emotional bond. So pick up that pen, let your heart guide your words, and watch as your love story unfolds through the power of written communication.

The Element of Anticipation: Adding Novelty and Excitement to Your Long Distance Relationship

Creating anticipation is a key ingredient in maintaining excitement and keeping the spark alive in a long distance relationship. The power of anticipation lies in the thrill and joy it brings, as well as the sense of anticipation that builds up before a special moment or surprise. By regularly incorporating surprises and moments of anticipation into your relationship, you can infuse it with a renewed sense of novelty and excitement.

The Benefits of Anticipation

Anticipation serves as a powerful tool for strengthening your connection with your partner. It creates a sense of excitement and eagerness, making every interaction feel more special. When you have something to look forward to, it can help alleviate the challenges of distance by providing a positive focus and reminding you of the love and commitment you share. Anticipation also fosters a spirit of adventure, as it encourages you to explore new ways to surprise and delight your partner.

Ways to Create Anticipation

1. Planning Surprise Trips: Surprise your partner with a planned visit, catching them off guard and igniting a sense of anticipation. Coordinate with their schedule and keep it a secret until the big reveal. The joy and excitement of seeing each other unexpectedly will create an unforgettable memory.

2. Organizing Surprise Activities: Surprise your partner by organizing special activities or experiences they would enjoy. It could be anything from a virtual cooking class together, arranging a surprise online game night with friends, or even planning a virtual movie night with synchronized streaming. These surprises will add a touch of excitement and show your thoughtfulness.

3. Sending Mystery Gifts: Consider sending your partner a mystery gift, where they won't know what it is until they open it. It could be a small token of love, a personalized item, or something related to their hobbies or interests. The anticipation of receiving an unknown gift will make them feel cherished and eagerly await its arrival.

How Anticipation Adds Novelty and Excitement

Anticipation injects a sense of novelty and excitement into your relationship, keeping it fresh and vibrant despite the physical distance. It breaks the monotony of day-to-day routines and creates moments to look forward to. By introducing surprises and cultivating anticipation, you are actively investing in the growth and vitality of your long distance love.

Understanding Your Partner's Desires and Preferences

Creating a sense of anticipation requires understanding and consideration of your partner's desires and preferences. Pay attention to their interests, hobbies, and dreams. Think about what they enjoy or have mentioned wanting to do. By tailoring surprises and moments of anticipation to their specific tastes, you show that you value their individuality and are dedicated to making them feel special.

Remember, the element of anticipation is not about grand gestures or expensive gifts; it is about thoughtfulness and the effort you put into creating meaningful surprises. By incorporating anticipation into your long distance relationship, you can reignite the spark and keep the excitement alive, reminding yourselves of the limitless possibilities that lie ahead. Stay tuned for more innovative ideas in the upcoming chapters to continue nurturing your long distance connection.

CHAPTER 8: PLANNING AHEAD: SETTING GOALS AND CREATING A CLEAR PATH FOR YOUR FUTURE TOGETHER

Identifying shared values and long-term goals

The foundation of any successful long distance relationship lies in the alignment of shared values and long-term goals. In this chapter, we will explore the importance of open and honest communication about individual aspirations and values, discuss ways to find common ground with your partner, and highlight the significance of shared values in building a future together.

When it comes to identifying shared values and long-term goals, open and honest communication is key. Take the time to have meaningful conversations with your partner about what truly matters to you. Share your dreams, desires, and the things that bring you joy. Discuss your values, beliefs, and the principles that guide your lives. By opening up to each other in this way, you will not only deepen your connection but also gain a better understanding of each other's perspectives.

It is essential to discuss how your values and long-term goals align with each other. Are there areas where your values overlap or complement each other? Are there differences that need to be addressed? These conversations will help you identify the areas of mutual interest and agreement, as well as potential areas of compromise.

Finding common ground is crucial in building a future together. Look for shared values and goals that you can both work towards. For example, if family is important to both of you, discuss your visions for starting a family and raising children. If career success is a shared value, explore how you can support and encourage each other's professional growth. By identifying these common areas, you can create a strong foundation for your relationship and ensure that you are moving in the same direction.

Recognize the importance of shared values in building a future together. Shared values provide a sense of unity and purpose, allowing you to navigate the challenges of a long distance relationship with confidence. When you and your partner share similar values, you are more likely to understand and support each other's decisions, even when you are physically apart. These shared values will guide your choices and actions, helping you stay connected and committed to your long-term goals.

Remember, the process of identifying shared values and long-term goals is ongoing. As you and your partner grow and evolve, it is important to continue having conversations about your aspirations and values. Keep an open mind and be willing to adapt and adjust your goals as needed. By staying connected and regularly reassessing your shared values, you can ensure that your relationship continues to flourish in the face of distance.

In the next sections, we will delve deeper into setting a

timeline and milestones, creating a roadmap, developing a financial plan, assessing compatibility, and embracing flexibility and adaptability. Each of these elements plays a crucial role in planning ahead and building a future together in a long distance relationship. Let's explore these topics more in-depth and empower you to take the necessary steps towards a strong and fulfilling future with your partner.

Establishing a timeline and milestones:

Setting specific milestones in the relationship is an essential step towards building a strong and fulfilling future together, especially in a long distance relationship. These milestones serve as guideposts that not only provide direction but also create a sense of progress and accomplishment. By discussing key moments and events, such as closing the distance or making major life decisions, you and your partner can work together towards a shared vision.

When setting these milestones, it is crucial to have open and honest communication about your individual aspirations and values. Take the time to discuss your dreams, ambitions, and desires for the future. Encourage each other to express your goals and aspirations without judgment or fear. By understanding each other's values and long-term goals, you can find common ground and align your visions for the future.

Creating a clear timeline for your relationship is another important aspect of planning ahead. This timeline should include specific milestones that mark significant moments in your journey together. For example, you might set a milestone for when you plan to close the distance or when you envision reaching a certain level of commitment. By establishing these milestones, you create a sense of direction and purpose, providing you with a roadmap towards your desired future.

To ensure the effectiveness of your timeline and milestones, it is essential to discuss them in detail with your partner. Take the time to understand each other's expectations and desires for these key moments. By openly communicating about these milestones, you can address any potential concerns or conflicts before they become bigger issues. Remember, flexibility and adaptability are vital in a long distance relationship, so be prepared to reassess and adjust your timeline as needed.

In addition to discussing significant events, it is equally important to celebrate the smaller milestones along the way. These could be as simple as reaching a certain number of months or years in your relationship, successfully navigating a challenging period of distance, or achieving personal growth together. By acknowledging and celebrating these milestones, you create a positive and motivating environment that strengthens your bond and keeps you focused on the future.

As you establish your timeline and milestones, keep in mind that they should be realistic and achievable. Set goals that are within reach and align with both of your capabilities and circumstances. While it's essential to dream big and aim high, it's equally important to set yourself up for success. Remember, your timeline is a tool to guide you, not a rigid structure that must be followed at all costs.

By setting specific milestones in your long distance relationship, discussing key moments and events, and creating a sense of direction and progress through your timeline, you lay the foundation for a future filled with love and commitment. Embrace this opportunity to dream together, plan together, and work towards a shared vision that encompasses both of your aspirations. With clear goals and a roadmap in place, you are equipped to overcome the distance and build a strong and lasting connection.

Creating a roadmap: Breaking down goals and milestones into actionable steps, discussing potential career paths and educational opportunities, and planning for relocation or joint projects as part of the roadmap.

Creating a clear path for your future together requires careful planning and setting achievable goals. In this section, we will explore how to break down your aspirations into actionable steps, discuss potential career paths and educational opportunities, and plan for relocation or joint projects as part of your roadmap.

Breaking down goals and milestones into actionable steps is essential for making progress in your long distance relationship. Start by identifying the specific goals you both want to achieve together, whether it's closing the distance, starting a family, or pursuing a shared passion. Once you have identified these goals, break them down into smaller, more manageable steps. For example, if your goal is to close the distance, your actionable steps may include researching job opportunities in each other's cities, exploring housing options, and saving a certain amount of money for moving expenses. By breaking down your goals, you can create a clear roadmap that outlines the necessary actions and timelines for each step.

Discussing potential career paths and educational opportunities is crucial for long-term planning. Take the time to openly communicate about your individual career aspirations and how they align with your shared future. Consider what career paths are available in each other's locations and explore educational opportunities that can enhance your professional growth. By discussing and supporting each other's career goals, you can ensure that your roadmap includes the necessary steps to achieve professional fulfillment alongside your relationship goals.

Planning for relocation or joint projects is another important aspect of creating a roadmap. If closing the distance is part of your long-term plan, discuss the logistics of relocating, such as finding suitable jobs in the new location, researching housing options, and considering the impact on your social and support networks.

Additionally, discuss any joint projects or ventures you may want to pursue together, whether it's starting a business, volunteering for a cause you both care about, or traveling the world. By incorporating these plans into your roadmap, you can create a shared vision for your future and make concrete plans to work towards it.

Remember, creating a roadmap requires flexibility and adaptability. Circumstances may change, and new opportunities may arise along the way. Be open-minded and willing to reassess your goals as needed. Regularly revisit and update your roadmap together, ensuring that it continues to align with your evolving aspirations and circumstances. Flexibility and adaptability are key in maintaining a successful long distance relationship and navigating the challenges that come with planning for the future.

In conclusion, creating a roadmap for your future together involves breaking down goals and milestones into actionable steps, discussing potential career paths and educational opportunities, and planning for relocation or joint projects. By taking these steps, you can establish a clear path forward and work towards a future that aligns with your shared vision. Stay committed to open and honest communication, and remember to remain flexible and adaptable as you navigate the journey together. With careful planning and a shared roadmap, you can build a strong foundation for a fulfilling and successful long distance relationship.

Developing a Financial Plan: Creating a Strong Foundation for Your Shared Future

Financial stability is a crucial aspect of any relationship, and long distance relationships are no exception. As you plan ahead and envision a future together, it's essential to develop a solid financial plan that aligns with your goals and aspirations. In this section, we will discuss the importance of savings and budgeting, long-term financial goals and investments, as well as preparing for any financial challenges that may arise along the way.

Savings and Budgeting: Building a Safety Net for Future Expenses

Saving money is not only financially responsible but also provides a sense of security for both you and your partner. Start by evaluating your current financial situation and determining how much you can realistically save each month. Set specific saving goals, whether it's for visits, future plans, or emergencies. Openly discuss your individual financial situations and explore ways to save collectively. Consider allocating a certain percentage of your income towards joint savings and create a budget that allows for regular contributions. Remember, even small amounts add up over time, so be consistent and disciplined in your saving habits.

Long-Term Financial Goals and Investments: Mapping Out Your Financial Future

Setting long-term financial goals is an important step in planning for your shared future. Discuss where you see yourselves financially in the next five, ten, or twenty years. Consider factors such as homeownership, investments, retirement plans, and other significant milestones you wish to achieve together. This conversation will help you establish a common vision and identify the steps needed to make those dreams a reality. Research investment options and consult with a financial advisor if necessary. By aligning your financial goals, you can work together towards a prosperous future.

Preparing for Financial Challenges: Navigating the Ups and Downs

Life is unpredictable, and financial challenges may arise unexpectedly. It's important to be prepared for them and develop strategies to overcome any bumps in the road. Discuss potential scenarios such as job loss, unexpected expenses, or changes in financial circumstances, and the impact they might have on your relationship. Explore contingency plans and brainstorm ways to support each other during difficult times. By openly addressing these challenges and finding solutions together, you will strengthen your bond and build resilience in the face of adversity.

Remember, financial planning is a continuous process that requires ongoing communication and adaptation. Regularly reassess your financial situation, evaluate your progress towards your goals, and make adjustments as needed. Celebrate milestones along the way, no matter how small, as they signify progress towards your shared future.

In conclusion, developing a financial plan is an essential part of setting goals and creating a clear path for your future together. By discussing savings and budgeting, considering long-term financial goals and investments, and preparing for any financial challenges, you are building a strong foundation for your shared life. Remember to communicate openly, be flexible, and support each other throughout this journey. With a solid financial plan in place, you can confidently navigate the ups and downs of a long distance relationship and work towards a prosperous and fulfilling future together.

Assessing Compatibility and Shared Responsibilities: Building a Solid Foundation for Your Future Together

In this section, we will explore the crucial aspects of compatibility and shared responsibilities in a long distance relationship. Evaluating your compatibility on topics such as family life and decision-making processes is essential for laying a strong foundation for your future together. Additionally, discussing the division of chores and shared responsibilities in a potential cohabitation scenario is vital to ensure a harmonious and balanced relationship. Finally, addressing any potential conflicts that may arise along the way and finding ways to compromise will help you navigate the challenges of merging your lives.

Evaluating compatibility on topics such as family life and

decision-making processes is crucial when envisioning a future together. Each individual brings their unique background, values, and expectations into a relationship. It is essential to have open and honest conversations about your families, traditions, and beliefs. Understanding each other's perspectives and finding common ground can help you navigate potential differences and create a shared vision for your future.

Furthermore, discussing the division of chores and shared responsibilities in a cohabitation scenario is necessary to establish a balanced and equitable partnership. Planning how household tasks, financial responsibilities, and decision-making processes will be divided can prevent future conflicts and ensure that both partners feel valued and heard. Consider each other's strengths, preferences, and availability when assigning responsibilities and be open to adjusting the division of labor as needed.

Addressing potential conflicts is an integral part of building a successful long distance relationship. As you plan for your future together, it is important to anticipate areas where conflicts may arise, such as lifestyle choices, career aspirations, or personal goals. By openly discussing these potential conflicts and finding ways to compromise, you can foster a sense of trust, understanding, and mutual support. Remember, compromise does not mean giving up your needs or desires; it means finding solutions that satisfy both partners' interests.

To address potential conflicts effectively, it is crucial to practice active listening, empathy, and respect. Seek to understand your partner's perspective and validate their feelings. Be willing to engage in open and honest discussions, even when it may be uncomfortable. By creating a safe space for dialogue and expressing your needs and concerns assertively yet empathetically, you can work together towards finding mutually beneficial solutions.

Remember, building a strong long distance relationship requires effort, patience, and effective communication. Assessing compatibility and shared responsibilities is a vital part of this journey. Openly discussing topics such as family life, decision-making processes, division of chores, and addressing potential conflicts will lay a solid foundation for your future together. By fostering understanding, compromise, and mutual support, you can navigate the challenges that come with merging your lives and build a relationship that thrives both in the distance and when you finally close the gap.

In the next section, we will explore the importance of flexibility and adaptability in a long distance relationship and how to embrace these qualities to ensure a resilient and fulfilling future together.

Flexibility and Adaptability: Navigating the Ever-Changing Path of Long Distance Love

In the intricate dance of a long distance relationship, it is essential to acknowledge that plans may change. Life has a way of throwing unexpected twists and turns our way, and being prepared to adapt is crucial in keeping your love story strong. This chapter will emphasize the importance of flexibility and adaptability, as well as provide practical advice on how to navigate the ever-changing path of long distance love.

Acknowledging that plans may change in a long distance relationship is the first step towards building a resilient partnership. We understand that circumstances beyond your control can arise, such as job opportunities, family obligations, or unforeseen events. By accepting that change is inevitable, you will be better equipped to handle unexpected situations with grace and resilience.

Emphasizing the importance of being flexible and adaptable is paramount in maintaining a healthy long distance relationship. It is crucial to remember that the dynamics of your relationship are not set in stone. As you and your partner grow individually and face new challenges, it is essential to be open to accommodating these changes. Flexibility allows for a smoother transition when unexpected events occur, enabling both of you to adapt and find creative solutions together.

Being open-minded and willing to reassess goals as circumstances evolve is a key component of navigating the long distance journey. Your roadmap and milestones may need to be adjusted along the way based on external factors or personal growth. We encourage you to have regular check-ins with your partner to discuss any changes or shifts in your aspirations. By keeping the lines of communication open, you can ensure that both of you are on the same page and can adapt your plans accordingly.

While it is important to remain committed to your shared goals, it is equally crucial to recognize when certain goals may no longer be feasible or suitable. As circumstances change, your priorities may shift, and it is essential to be willing to reassess and adapt your plans accordingly. This can be an opportunity for growth and exploration, as you and your partner discover new possibilities and redefine your future together.

Remember that flexibility and adaptability go hand in hand with trust and communication. By fostering a strong foundation of trust, you can approach any changes or uncertainties with a sense of security. Regular and open communication will enable you to navigate these challenges together, ensuring that both of you feel heard and understood throughout the process.

In conclusion, flexibility and adaptability are paramount in a long distance relationship. By acknowledging that plans may change, emphasizing the importance of being flexible and adaptable, and being open-minded and willing to reassess goals as circumstances evolve, you can navigate the ever-changing path of long distance love with confidence. Embrace the unexpected, communicate openly, and remember that your love can withstand any twists and turns that come your way.

CHAPTER 9: MAKING VISITS COUNT: MAXIMIZING THE QUALITY TIME YOU HAVE IN PERSON

CHAPTER 9: MAKING VISITS COUNT: MAXIMIZING THE QUALITY TIME YOU HAVE IN PERSON

Planning Ahead: Coordinating schedules and logistics for the visit to ensure smooth coordination

When it comes to visiting your partner in a long distance relationship, proper planning is key to maximizing the quality time you have together. Coordinating schedules and logistics in advance will help ensure a smooth and hassle-free visit. Here are some tips to help you plan ahead effectively:

1. Coordinate schedules: Before making any arrangements, take the time to synchronize your schedules with your partner. Identify a time that works best for both of you, considering work commitments, personal obligations, and any other factors that may affect your availability.

2. Book flights and accommodations: Once you have determined the dates for your visit, book your flights and accommodations as early as possible. This will not only give you more options but also help you secure better deals. Consider using travel websites or apps to compare prices and find the most convenient options for

your budget.

3. Make necessary arrangements: Besides flights and accommodations, think about other arrangements you may need to make in advance. For example, if you plan on renting a car, reserving tickets for a concert or show, or making dinner reservations at a popular restaurant, it's best to do so ahead of time to avoid disappointment.

Creating a List of Activities or Experiences: Planning meaningful moments together

Making the most out of your time together means having a list of activities or experiences you both want to enjoy during your visit. By discussing and planning these activities in advance, you can ensure that you make the most of every moment. Here's how to create a comprehensive list:

1. Brainstorm together: Sit down with your partner and brainstorm a list of activities or experiences you both have been longing to try or places you want to visit. This can include anything from going for a hike, exploring local landmarks, trying new restaurants, or even just having a cozy movie night at home.

2. Prioritize and organize: Once you have a list of ideas, prioritize them based on your interests and the time available. Consider any budget constraints or time limitations that may affect what you can realistically achieve during your visit. Organize the activities in a way that allows for a balance between excitement and relaxation.

3. Be flexible: While having a plan is essential, remember to be flexible and open to spontaneous moments as well. Leave room for surprises and unexpected adventures that may arise during your time together. Sometimes, the most cherished memories are made when you least expect them.

Considering Constraints and Limitations: Planning accordingly for a successful visit

When planning your visit, it's important to consider any constraints or limitations that may impact your time together. By taking these factors into account, you can plan accordingly and ensure a successful and enjoyable visit. Here are some things to keep in mind:

1. Time constraints: If you have a limited amount of time for your visit, be realistic about what you can accomplish. Avoid overwhelming yourselves with too many activities and focus on quality over quantity. Remember, it's better to have fewer meaningful experiences than rush through a packed schedule.

2. Budget limitations: Financial considerations can also impact your visit. Discuss your budget with your partner and make sure to plan activities that align with your financial capabilities. Look for free or low-cost options for entertainment and consider cooking meals together instead of dining out every night.

3. Physical limitations: If either you or your partner have any physical limitations or health concerns, plan activities that accommodate those needs. For example, if one of you has difficulty walking long distances, choose destinations that are accessible and offer alternatives like wheelchair accessibility or guided tours.

By planning ahead, creating a list of activities, and considering any constraints or limitations, you can make the most of your visits and create lasting memories with your partner. Remember, the key is to focus on quality time and meaningful experiences that strengthen the bond between you and your loved one, even if the physical distance separates you.

CHAPTER 9: MAKING VISITS COUNT: MAXIMIZING THE QUALITY TIME YOU HAVE IN PERSON

Open communication: Ensuring both partners feel heard, understood, and respected

In any long distance relationship, open communication is essential, especially when it comes to making the most of your visits together. It's important to have a discussion about your expectations, desires, and boundaries for the visit. This will help you align your goals and ensure that both partners feel heard, understood, and respected during this precious time.

Start by sharing your thoughts and preferences on how to spend your limited time together. Each of you may have different ideas and activities in mind, so having an open conversation can help you find common ground. Maybe one of you wants to explore the local attractions, while the other prefers quiet evenings at home. By discussing these preferences, you can come up with a plan that incorporates both of your desires.

During this conversation, it's crucial to actively listen to each other. Let your partner express their thoughts and feelings without interruption, and make sure they know you value their input. Remember that open communication is a two-way street, so be willing to share your own preferences and listen to their responses as well.

Sometimes, compromises may be necessary to ensure both partners have a fulfilling visit. Maybe you want to spend one day exploring the city, but your partner would like to visit a museum. Seek a middle ground where you can alternate between activities that appeal to both of you. Compromising allows you to create a balance and ensure that neither of you feels left out or ignored.

Additionally, it's important to keep in mind that expectations can differ from reality. While you may have envisioned the perfect visit, unforeseen circumstances or external factors may affect your plans. By maintaining open communication, you can address any unexpected changes or challenges as a team, finding alternative solutions and adjusting your expectations accordingly.

Lastly, remember that open communication extends beyond discussing plans for your visit. It also involves emotional connection and vulnerability. Take the time to openly express your feelings, fears, and hopes for the future. This will deepen your bond and strengthen your relationship, even during the limited time you have together.

By having open and honest discussions about your expectations, desires, and boundaries, you can ensure that your visit is filled with meaningful moments and cherished memories. Open communication is the foundation that allows both partners to feel heard, understood, and respected, making your time together truly special. Together, you can align your goals, make compromises when necessary, and create an atmosphere of love and understanding.

Quality over quantity:

In long distance relationships, every moment spent together is precious. Rather than trying to fill every minute with activities, it is essential to emphasize meaningful experiences that foster intimacy and emotional connection. By valuing quiet and intimate moments over a packed schedule of outings, you can truly maximize the quality time you have in person.

When you are fortunate enough to be physically together, it is crucial to be fully present and engaged in each moment. Put away distractions and focus on each other. This means setting aside time to have deep conversations, listen attentively, and make eye contact. By giving each other undivided attention, you can strengthen your emotional bond and create lasting memories.

Prioritizing intimacy is key during your visits. While it can be tempting to plan elaborate dates and grand gestures, remember that the most significant moments often come from simple acts of love and connection. Enjoy a quiet dinner together, take a walk hand in hand, or snuggle up and watch a movie. These intimate moments allow you to savor each other's presence and deepen your connection on an emotional level.

Valuing quality over quantity also means recognizing that it's okay to have downtime during your visit. It's not necessary to fill every minute with activities to make the most of your time together. In fact, leaving space for relaxation and reflection can enhance the overall experience. Take advantage of the opportunity to slow down and enjoy each other's company without feeling pressured to constantly be on the go. Appreciate the simple joys of just being together.

Another aspect of prioritizing quality over quantity is understanding that the strength of your relationship lies in the emotional connection you share, not the number of activities you check off a list. While it's natural to want to create memorable experiences during your visits, remember that the true value comes from the love and support you offer each other. Cherish the moments of vulnerability, laughter, and shared dreams. These are the experiences that will leave a lasting impact on your relationship.

To truly maximize the quality time you have during visits, it's essential to be intentional in your actions and choices. Take the time to plan activities that align with both of your interests and values. By incorporating elements that are meaningful to both partners, you can create experiences that resonate deeply and strengthen your connection.

In summary, making the most of your visits in a long distance relationship is about prioritizing quality over quantity. Emphasize meaningful experiences, be fully present and engaged in each moment, prioritize intimacy and emotional connection, and value quiet and intimate moments together. Remember, it's not about filling every minute with activities, but about creating lasting memories and deepening your bond. By focusing on the quality of your time together, you can make every visit count.

Incorporating their world: Engaging in activities that your partner enjoys, exploring their favorite places and sharing their hobbies or interests, meeting their friends and family to deepen your understanding of their life, and making an effort to learn more about their culture or traditions.

One of the most rewarding aspects of being in a long distance relationship is the opportunity to immerse yourself in your partner's world during visits. By engaging in activities that your partner enjoys and exploring their favorite places, you not only create lasting memories together but also gain a deeper understanding of their life. In this section, we will discuss how incorporating your partner's world into your visits can strengthen your connection and enrich your overall long distance love story.

Engaging in activities that your partner enjoys is a wonderful way to show your support and interest in their life. Whether it's joining them for a hike, trying out a new hobby together, or attending a concert they've been excited about, participating in their favorite activities will not only bring you closer but also allow you to experience their passions firsthand. By stepping into their world, you demonstrate your willingness to be a part of their life, even when you're physically apart.

Exploring your partner's favorite places is another meaningful way to connect during visits. Take the time to visit the local spots they hold dear, whether it's a charming café, a picturesque park, or a hidden gem in their city. By experiencing these places together, you'll gain insight into their daily life and create shared memories in familiar surroundings. Additionally, consider asking your partner to show you around their neighborhood, introducing you to the places and people that have shaped who they are today.

Meeting your partner's friends and family is a significant step towards deepening your understanding of their life. These individuals play a vital role in your partner's support system, and getting to know them will provide valuable insights into your partner's values, upbringing, and relationships. Engage in conversations, ask questions, and show genuine interest in their lives. By forming connections with the important people in your partner's world, you'll not only strengthen your bond with them but also demonstrate your commitment to being a part of their broader network.

To truly incorporate your partner's world into your visits, make an effort to learn more about their culture or traditions. This could involve trying traditional dishes, attending cultural events or celebrations, or even learning a few phrases in their language. By immersing yourself in their cultural experiences, you demonstrate respect and appreciation for their background, fostering a deeper sense of connection and understanding.

Remember, the purpose of incorporating your partner's world

into your visits is not to lose your identity or sacrifice your own interests, but rather to create a harmonious blend of both your lives. It's about finding common ground, discovering new experiences together, and appreciating the unique aspects that each of you brings to the relationship. By embracing your partner's world, you'll not only strengthen your bond but also lay the foundation for a future where both of you can thrive as individuals while remaining connected as a couple.

In the next section, we will discuss the importance of balancing alone time and together time during visits, ensuring that both partners' needs for personal space are respected.

Balancing Alone Time and Together Time: Finding Harmony in Your Long Distance Relationship

Throughout your long distance relationship, it is essential to recognize and respect each other's need for personal space. While spending quality time together is crucial, honoring individual needs for alone time is equally important. Balancing these two aspects can help create a healthy and thriving dynamic during your visits. In this section, we will explore strategies to find the right balance and communicate effectively about alone time and together time.

Recognizing and respecting each other's need for personal space: During visits, it's natural to want to spend every waking moment together, but it's vital to remember that both partners still have individual lives and interests. Recognizing and respecting each other's need for personal space allows for a healthier and more fulfilling connection. Understand that alone time doesn't reflect a lack of love or interest; rather, it helps recharge and maintain a sense of self.

Finding a healthy balance between spending quality time together and honoring individual needs:
While it's important to make the most of your limited time

together, it's equally crucial to find a balance that respects both partners' desires and needs. By prioritizing quality over quantity, you can create memorable experiences while leaving room for personal growth and rejuvenation. Recognize that finding this balance may require compromise and open communication.

Discussing and establishing boundaries around alone time and alone activities:

Clear and open communication is key when it comes to balancing alone time and together time. Discuss with your partner your individual expectations and the boundaries you each have regarding alone time and alone activities. This could include agreeing on specific periods of the day when you can have your own space, engaging in solo hobbies, or simply enjoying some quiet time. Establishing these boundaries will help ensure that both partners feel comfortable and respected.

Communicating openly about any feelings of suffocation or loneliness:

During visits, it's possible to feel overwhelmed by constant togetherness or, conversely, experience moments of loneliness due to the impending separation. It is crucial to communicate openly and honestly with your partner about these emotions. If you need some alone time or are feeling suffocated, express your feelings respectfully and give your partner a chance to understand. Similarly, if you're feeling lonely, let your partner know, so they can provide the emotional support you need.

By finding a healthy balance between alone time and together time, you can foster a stronger connection and overall satisfaction in your long distance relationship. Remember, it's essential to recognize and respect each other's need for personal space, while still prioritizing quality time together. Communicate openly about expectations and boundaries, and be responsive to each other's emotions. With these strategies in place, you can make the most out of your visits and create lasting memories together.

Creating Lasting Memories: Capturing Moments of Togetherness and Connection

In this chapter, we will explore the importance of creating lasting memories during your visits. These memories serve as cherished reminders of the love and connection you share, even when you are physically apart. By capturing special moments through photographs, videos, or mementos, discussing ways to preserve these memories, finding creative ways to commemorate your time together, and reflecting on them during periods of separation, you can maintain a sense of closeness and warmth in your long distance relationship.

Capturing Special Moments:

During your visits, take the time to capture the moments that make your heart flutter. Whether it's a romantic sunset stroll, a cozy night in by the fireplace, or a fun adventure exploring a new city, preserve these special moments through photographs, videos, or even small mementos. These tangible reminders will allow you to relive and cherish these experiences long after you've said your goodbyes.

Discussing Ways to Preserve Memories:

Communication is key in maintaining a strong long distance relationship, and this also applies to preserving memories. Talk with your partner about how you can keep these memories alive during future times apart. Consider creating a shared photo album online, where you can both contribute pictures from your visits. Explore the idea of recording videos together, sharing your thoughts and feelings about your time spent together. By discussing and implementing these ideas, you'll cultivate a shared archive of precious memories that can be revisited whenever you need a reminder of the love you share.

Finding Creative Ways to Commemorate Your Time Together:

In addition to capturing moments through traditional means, consider finding unique ways to commemorate your visits. Perhaps you can exchange small gifts that represent a special memory or inside joke from your time together. Create a scrapbook or a memory box filled with tokens and keepsakes from your visits, such as movie tickets, handwritten notes, or pressed flowers. By putting thought and effort into these commemorative gestures, you are not only creating lasting memories but also strengthening the bond between you and your partner.

Reflecting on Memories during Periods of Separation:

When you find yourself apart again, take the time to reflect on the memories you've created together. Look through the photographs, watch the videos, or revisit the mementos you've collected. Allow these memories to bring a smile to your face and fill your heart with warmth. Reflecting on these cherished moments will help you maintain a sense of closeness even when the miles between you seem unbearable. It serves as a reminder that despite the physical distance, your love is real and enduring.

We understand the power of creating lasting memories in a long distance relationship. By capturing special moments, discussing ways to preserve those memories, finding creative ways to commemorate your time together, and reflecting on them during periods of separation, you can strengthen the bond with your partner and keep the flame of love burning brightly. Remember, the memories you create today will be the foundation of the love story you continue to write together, no matter how far apart you may be.

CHAPTER 10: THRIVING IN THE DISTANCE: INSPIRATIONAL STORIES OF COUPLES WHO HAVE SUCCESSFULLY MAINTAINED STRONG LONG DISTANCE RELATIONSHIPS

Thriving in a long distance relationship is no easy feat, but maintaining open and honest communication is key to overcoming the challenges that distance presents. In this section, we will explore the importance of consistent and frequent communication, effective communication strategies, overcoming communication challenges, sharing emotions and aspirations, and utilizing technology to enhance communication.

Consistent and frequent communication is vital to staying connected in a long distance relationship. When you are physically apart, communication becomes the lifeline that keeps your bond strong. It's important to make a conscious effort to communicate regularly with your partner, whether it's through video calls, phone calls, or written letters. This consistent communication helps bridge the physical distance and allows you to stay emotionally connected.

Effective communication strategies are essential for long distance couples. Scheduled video calls can create a sense of routine and anticipation, providing you both with something to look forward to. Written letters can be a heartfelt way of expressing your thoughts and feelings, allowing for deep and meaningful conversations. It's also important to find a communication method that works best for both of you, taking into consideration factors such as time zones and language barriers.

Overcoming communication challenges is an integral part of thriving in a long distance relationship. Language barriers can be navigated by using translation apps or learning each other's languages together. Time zone differences can be managed by finding overlapping times that work for both of your schedules and being flexible with your availability. By actively addressing and finding solutions to these challenges, you can ensure that communication remains a priority in your relationship.

Sharing emotions, aspirations, and daily life updates is crucial in strengthening the emotional connection in a long distance relationship. It's important to create a safe space where both partners feel comfortable expressing their feelings and thoughts. This can be done through regular check-ins and open conversations about how you're feeling, what you're excited about, and any challenges you may be facing. Sharing these aspects of your life helps build a deeper understanding and connection between you and your partner.

Utilizing technology is a powerful tool to enhance communication in a long distance relationship. Messaging apps can provide an easy and convenient way to stay connected throughout the day, even with time zone differences. Shared calendars can help you keep track of each other's schedules and plan future visits. It's important to embrace the technological resources available to you and incorporate them into your communication routine.

By prioritizing open and honest communication, utilizing effective strategies, overcoming challenges, sharing emotions and aspirations, and embracing technology, you can thrive in your long distance relationship. Remember, communication is the foundation that allows love to transcend distance.

Building trust is essential for any relationship, but it becomes even more crucial in a long distance relationship where physical distance can sometimes create doubts and insecurities. Trust serves as the foundation that holds a long distance relationship together, providing a sense of security and confidence in each other's commitment and loyalty. In this section, we will explore various aspects of trust in long distance relationships, from establishing trust to handling jealousy and insecurity, and even rebuilding trust after breaches or misunderstandings.

To establish trust in a long distance relationship, transparency, reliability, and accountability are key. It's important to be open and honest with your partner about your feelings, fears, and expectations. Clear communication plays a significant role in building trust, ensuring that both partners are on the same page and understand each other's needs and boundaries. Consistency is also vital in demonstrating reliability and dependability. By fulfilling promises and following through on commitments, you show your partner that they can rely on you, regardless of the physical distance between you.

Jealousy and insecurities are common challenges that can arise in a long distance relationship. However, cultivating trust in oneself and the relationship can help manage these emotions. It's essential to recognize that jealousy is often rooted in fear and insecurity. By focusing on building self-confidence and self-esteem, you can combat these negative emotions. Practicing open and honest communication about your insecurities with your partner can foster understanding and support, allowing both of you to work through these challenges together.

Trust-building activities and exercises can also strengthen the bond between you and your partner. For example, sharing passwords can foster a sense of transparency and openness. By granting each other access to your personal accounts, such as social media or email, you create an atmosphere of trust and demonstrate your commitment to honesty. Introducing trusted friends or family members to each other can also help solidify trust by expanding your support network and showing that your partner is an important part of your life.

However, there may be instances where trust is compromised. Rebuilding trust after breaches or misunderstandings requires time, patience, and consistent effort from both partners. It's crucial to address the issue openly and honestly, allowing for open dialogue and understanding. Apologizing sincerely, taking responsibility for one's actions, and working towards positive changes can help rebuild trust. It's essential to remember that rebuilding trust is a process and may take time, but with commitment and effort, it is possible to restore the bond.

In summary, trust is the pillar of any successful long distance relationship. Establishing trust through transparency, reliability, and accountability is vital. Communicating openly and honestly, being consistent in your actions, and fulfilling promises are key elements in building trust. Managing jealousy and insecurities by cultivating trust in oneself and the relationship can help overcome these challenges. Engaging in trust-building activities and exercises can solidify the bond between partners. Finally, in cases of breaches or misunderstandings, rebuilding trust requires open communication, sincere apologies, and a commitment to positive change. By prioritizing trust, you can strengthen the foundation of your long distance relationship and ensure its longevity.

Fostering a Positive Mindset and Managing Jealousy and Insecurities: Keys to Emotional Well-being in a Long Distance Relationship

Long distance relationships can be challenging, filled with moments of doubt, insecurity, and jealousy. However, fostering a positive mindset and effectively managing these emotions is crucial for maintaining emotional well-being and the overall health of your relationship. In this section, we will explore the importance of nurturing a positive attitude towards your distance relationship, recognizing and addressing jealous thoughts and feelings, coping strategies for dealing with jealousy, boosting self-esteem and self-confidence, and practicing empathy and understanding towards your partner's emotions.

Maintaining a positive attitude towards your long distance relationship is vital for its success. It's normal to have moments of sadness or longing due to the physical separation, but focusing on the positives can help you stay motivated and hopeful. Remind yourself of the reasons why you chose to embark on this journey together and the love that binds you. Celebrate the milestones and achievements, no matter how small, and view the distance as an opportunity for personal growth and strengthening your bond.

Jealousy is a natural emotion that can arise in any relationship, especially when distance is involved. It's important to recognize and address these feelings openly and honestly with your partner. Ignoring or suppressing jealous thoughts can lead to resentment and insecurity. Communicate your insecurities calmly and constructively, sharing how you feel without blaming your partner. By discussing these concerns, you can work together to find solutions and reassurance.

When it comes to coping with jealousy, reframing your perspective can be immensely helpful. Instead of dwelling on negative thoughts or comparing your relationship to others, focus on the unique aspects that make your love special. Trust in the strength of your connection and remind yourself of the commitment you both share. Engaging in hobbies, practicing self-care, and maintaining a fulfilling life outside of your relationship can also alleviate feelings of jealousy by increasing your sense of self-worth and individuality.

Boosting your self-esteem and self-confidence is essential in any relationship, but particularly in a long distance one. Remind yourself of your worth and the qualities that make you a loving and deserving partner. Take time to pursue personal goals and passions, as achieving your own dreams can contribute to your overall happiness and sense of fulfillment. Surround yourself with supportive friends and family who uplift and encourage you.

Practicing empathy and understanding towards your partner's feelings is crucial for creating a safe and nurturing environment. Recognize that they may also be experiencing moments of insecurity and vulnerability. Listen attentively to their concerns, validate their emotions, and offer reassurance. Remember that maintaining open and empathetic communication fosters trust and strengthens the emotional connection between you both.

In conclusion, fostering a positive mindset and effectively managing jealousy and insecurities are vital for maintaining emotional well-being in a long distance relationship. Nurturing a positive attitude, recognizing and addressing jealous thoughts and feelings, coping strategies such as open communication and reframing perspectives, boosting self-esteem and self-confidence, and practicing empathy towards your partner's emotions are all essential components of thriving in the distance. By implementing these strategies, you can navigate the challenges with grace and create a strong foundation for your long distance love story.

Setting and Respecting Boundaries: Striking the Perfect Balance in Your Long Distance Relationship

In a long distance relationship, it's crucial to understand the significance of personal space and individual needs. While the distance may naturally create a level of independence, it's important to strike a healthy balance between independence and togetherness. This is where setting and respecting boundaries come into play.

When we talk about boundaries, we're referring to the limits and guidelines that you establish within your relationship to ensure both partners feel comfortable and respected. Boundaries help avoid emotional burnout and maintain a sense of autonomy, which is essential for a healthy and fulfilling long distance relationship.

Understanding your personal space and individual needs is the first step toward setting effective boundaries. Take some time to reflect on what makes you feel secure, respected, and fulfilled in your relationship. Consider your preferences for alone time, social interactions, and personal activities. By having a clear understanding of your own needs, you'll be better equipped to communicate them to your partner.

Setting boundaries is not about creating barriers or restrictions, but rather about creating an environment where both partners can thrive. It's important to communicate your boundaries effectively and create mutual understandings. Start by openly discussing your needs and expectations with your partner. Be honest about what makes you feel comfortable and what doesn't. Remember, communication is key in any relationship, especially in a long distance one.

Equally important is identifying and respecting your partner's boundaries. Just as you have your own needs, so does your partner. Take the time to listen, understand, and acknowledge their boundaries. Show empathy and respect for their individuality. By fostering an open and supportive environment, you'll create a strong foundation for trust and understanding.

Negotiating compromises is another vital aspect of setting boundaries. No two individuals are exactly alike, and finding a balance that suits both partners requires give-and-take. Each partner should be willing to make adjustments and accommodate the needs of the other. Flexibility is key when it comes to finding a healthy balance between alone time and quality time together.

Remember, boundaries are not set in stone. They may evolve over time as you and your partner grow and change. It's important to reassess and adjust your boundaries periodically to ensure they continue to meet your needs and align with your relationship's dynamics.

By setting and respecting boundaries, you'll create a solid framework for a healthy and thriving long distance relationship. You'll feel more secure, respected, and fulfilled, knowing that both you and your partner have established guidelines that foster a sense of independence and togetherness. So, take a moment to reflect on your personal needs, communicate them openly, and be open to negotiating compromises. By doing so, you'll find the perfect balance within your long distance love story.

Developing Coping Strategies for Times of Loneliness and Emotional Disconnection: Navigating the Challenges of Distance

Loneliness is an inevitable part of being in a long distance relationship. The physical separation can often lead to feelings of emptiness, sadness, and longing. However, it's important to recognize and accept these emotions as normal and valid. By acknowledging them, you can begin to develop coping strategies that will help you navigate through the challenging periods of loneliness and emotional disconnection.

One effective coping technique is to engage in hobbies and activities that bring you joy and fulfillment. Find something you are passionate about and dedicate time to it regularly. Whether it's painting, playing a musical instrument, or practicing yoga, immersing yourself in activities that you love can help distract your mind from the loneliness and provide a sense of purpose and fulfillment.

Another valuable way to combat loneliness is by connecting with friends and family. Surrounding yourself with loved ones who understand and support your relationship can make all the difference. Schedule regular video calls or even plan virtual hangouts where you can catch up and share experiences. Their presence and understanding will provide comfort and remind you that you are not alone in this journey.

Practicing self-care is essential for maintaining your emotional well-being during times of loneliness. Take the time to nurture yourself physically, mentally, and emotionally. Engage in activities that promote self-reflection and self-improvement, such as journaling, meditation, or taking relaxing baths. Additionally, prioritize your physical health by exercising regularly, eating nutritious meals, and getting enough sleep. Taking care of yourself will not only boost your mood but also make you feel more resilient in the face of emotional challenges.

When experiencing emotional disconnection in your long distance relationship, it's crucial to address the issue openly and honestly. Communicate with your partner about your feelings, concerns, and needs. By expressing your emotions and discussing possible solutions together, you can work towards reconnecting and strengthening your bond.

In times of intense loneliness or emotional disconnection, seeking support from trusted individuals can be immensely helpful. Reach out to friends, family members, or even online communities who have experienced similar challenges. Sharing your feelings with someone who understands can provide comfort, advice, and reassurance. Additionally, if the emotional strain becomes overwhelming, don't hesitate to seek professional counseling. A therapist can offer guidance and tools to navigate the complexities of long distance relationships while prioritizing your mental health.

Creating a support system with your partner is also vital in combatting loneliness and emotional disconnection. Together, brainstorm ways to stay connected and support each other during difficult times. This can include setting aside dedicated time for meaningful conversations, planning virtual movie nights, or even sending surprise care packages. By actively working together to overcome the challenges of distance, you'll feel more united and resilient as a couple.

In conclusion, developing coping strategies for times of loneliness and emotional disconnection is essential in thriving in a long distance relationship. By recognizing and accepting these emotions, engaging in fulfilling activities, connecting with loved ones, practicing self-care, communicating openly, seeking support when needed, and creating a support system with your partner, you can navigate the challenges of distance with strength and resilience. Remember, you are not alone in this journey, and with the right strategies, you can maintain a strong and fulfilling long distance relationship.

Finding creative ways to connect and create intimacy through technology is a crucial aspect of thriving in a long distance relationship. In this section, we will explore various techniques and ideas that can help bridge the physical gap and maintain a strong emotional connection despite the distance.

Utilizing virtual date nights and activities is an excellent way to recreate shared experiences and spend quality time together. Thanks to technology, you can now watch movies together, cook together, or even play online games as if you were in the same room. This allows you to enjoy each other's company and create lasting memories, despite the miles between you.

Engaging in shared hobbies or projects is another effective strategy to foster connection and strengthen your bond. Whether it's painting, writing, or learning a new language, finding a hobby that both of you can pursue individually and discuss together creates a sense of shared purpose and mutual growth. It also provides an opportunity to support and cheer each other on from afar.

Exploring different ways to express love and affection remotely is essential for keeping the romance alive in a long distance relationship. While physical touch may not be possible, there are numerous ways to show your partner how much you care. Sending heartfelt messages, voice recordings, or even surprise video calls can make your loved one feel cherished and valued. Additionally, leaving little love notes or sending care packages filled with thoughtful gifts can bring joy and excitement to your relationship.

Incorporating surprise gestures and gifts is a fantastic way to maintain the excitement and keep the spark alive in your long distance relationship. Surprise your partner with a favorite book, a handwritten letter, or a thoughtful memento that symbolizes your love. These gestures not only remind your partner of your affection but also make them feel special and appreciated.

Technology can also facilitate shared experiences despite the distance. Use video calls to have virtual meals together, go on virtual tours of museums or landmarks, or even take a walk together while sharing the screen. These activities create a sense of togetherness and allow you to explore the world together, even if you can't physically be there.

By utilizing these creative ways to connect and create intimacy through technology, you can bridge the physical gap in your long distance relationship and foster a deeper emotional connection. Remember, it's the little gestures and shared experiences that make a significant impact on the strength and growth of your relationship, regardless of the distance between you. Embrace the opportunities that technology offers and let it be a powerful tool in nurturing your love and keeping the flame burning bright.